Harini Iyengar was called to the Bar in 1999, as a seven-months-pregnant, young, single mother. She has now spent 20 years practising Employment, Public and Commercial law at 11KBW Chambers, and is ranked as a leading barrister in Employment and Education law in the legal directories "Chambers & Partners" and "Legal 500". Harini is a Governing Bencher at the Honourable Society of the Inner Temple and sits on the Steering Group of the Temple Women's Forum and the Bar Council Retention Panel of the Equality Committee. As a legal expert, she gave evidence to the House of Commons Inquiry into high heels and workplace dress codes, and is a regular commentator on television, radio, newspapers, magazines and online.

Outside her professional practice, Harini is an Independent Governor of London Metropolitan University. In 2015, she became a founding member of the Women's Equality Party, and is now an elected National Spokesperson and Member of Policy Committee, who has stood for Parliament, the Greater London Assembly, Hackney Mayor and two local council seats. Harini is the lone parent of three children.

A Practical Guide to the Law of Gender Pay Gap Reporting

A Practical Guide to the Law of Gender Pay Gap Reporting

Harini Iyengar
MA (Oxon), BCL (Oxon)

Law Brief Publishing

Published 2019 by Law Brief Publishing, an imprint of Law Brief Publishing Ltd, 30 The Parks, Minehead, Somerset, TA24 8BT

www.lawbriefpublishing.com

Paperback: 978-1-911035-94-7

This book is dedicated to all the working mothers

who every day put food on the table,

both literally and metaphorically

FOREWORD BY THE RIGHT HONOURABLE DAME ELIZABETH GLOSTER

Harini Iyengar is to be congratulated on the production of this excellent – and eminently readable – *Practical Guide to the Law of Gender Pay Gap Reporting*. As she herself says, the book is fundamentally a book about the enforcement of equal pay law. It therefore rightly focuses on the complex equality of terms provisions in the Equality Act 2010 (which provide the right to equal pay for equal work in Britain) and provides incisive guidance as to how employers should comply with the Equality Act 2010 (Gender Pay Gap Information) Regulations 2017.

But this book offers much more than a mere analysis of statutory rules and regulations. Harini gives us what she describes as "the cultural, moral and legal origins of equal pay rules". This affords her the opportunity of sharing with us, for example, her personal, but, as a practitioner in the field, nonetheless interesting and informed, views on the past failings of Parliament to introduce a comprehensive and clear regime governing equal pay for women. For example, she considers that the unwieldy and technically complex regime created by the Equal Pay Act 1970 has been a major contributor to the poor practical enforcement of women's rights to equal pay and the persistence of the gender pay gap. She expresses her view that "the root of the complex procedural and substantive barriers to practical enforcement of the right to equal pay is the legal fiction of the sex equality clause, which is implied into the contract of employment by automatic operation of law". And she cannot resist from concluding that "This legal fiction was created by a male-dominated Parliament in the Equal Pay Act 1970, and transported, almost unchanged in substance although set out more cogently, and updated to reflect caselaw, by another male-dominated Parliament, into the Equality Act 2010."! It is glimpses such as these of Harini the feminist politician and activist, which make this book a delight to read.

The book also provides an interesting insight into the fact that, because the Regulations focus solely on gender equality, and do not address pay gaps created by any other legally-protected characteristics under the Equality Act (e.g. age, disability, gender reassignment, marriage and civil partnership, pregnancy and maternity, race, religion or belief, or sexual orientation) or by socio-economic origins, the figures obtained under the reporting regime will not inform employers or employees exactly why certain groups of women employees may be earning less in their workforce. Thus, the regime "will not reveal any subtleties affecting women's training, development or career progression within the organisation and it will not demonstrate whether pay inequality arises from any other factors of intersectional disadvantage, for example, pregnancy or maternity, childcare or domestic responsibilities, race, disability, lone parent status, domestic violence, or sexual orientation". As Harini suggests, the failure of the Regulations to foster an intersectional approach, capable of acknowledging the intersections of privilege and disadvantage in real women's lives, may well undermine their practical utility and effect.

The struggle for equality of pay for women has had a long history. Of course, equality of educational opportunity for women has likewise been a lengthy story – and problems still exist today; see, for example, my partially dissenting judgment in *Chief Inspector of Education, Children's Services and Skills v The Interim Executive Board of Al-Hijra School.* But there is limited practical use in an equal education, if women are not in reality afforded equality of pay and opportunity in the subsequent workplace.

In her book, Harini refers to some aspects of the history of women's struggle for equal pay. If I had been its author, I might (for obvious reasons shortly to be revealed) have mentioned the role played the Equal Pay Campaign Committee (EPCC), a women's group, which was founded in 1941 with representatives from a number of women's organisations, which, during the 1920s, had begun to campaign for equal pay for women, only for the Depression to see women workers blamed for unemployment amongst men and many trades unions consequently become hostile to the issue. During World War II, the issue of women's pay inequity came to the fore, with lower settlements being offered to women under the Personal Injuries (Civilians) Scheme. This scheme was successfully overturned as a result of campaigning by women's organisations such as the Women Power Committee, the National Association of Women Civil Servants and the British Federation of Business & Professional Women, amongst others.

Attention was then turned to extending equal pay more generally and the EPCC was formed. It quickly instigated parliamentary debates and a Royal Commission on Equal Pay was announced largely due to its efforts, although initially the EPCC opposed the establishment of the Royal Commission because it took the view that there would be "consequent delay in settling the question" and that "more than enough evidence has been given already".

In 1946, the Royal Commission concluded tentatively that women in teaching and certain grades of the civil service might benefit from equal pay. Apparently, even these very modest proposals were rejected as inflationary by the Labour Government. Three of the four women on the Commission thought equal pay should be extended to women in industry and produced a minority report; their dissent makes an amusing read for anyone interested in the history of male attitudes to women in the workplace. The EPCC organised publicity and public meetings to support the implementation of the Royal Commission's conclusions on equal pay and started a national (but ultimately unsuccessful) campaign for more extensive equal pay.

My mother-in-law, Nina Popplewell, a suffragette, civil servant and a member of various women's organisations such as the Fawcett Society, whom I, sadly, never met, became Secretary of the EPCC in 1947 and was active in the campaign. She, like Harini, would have been appalled at the length of time it has taken to achieve even the current state of play where, although notionally women have the right to equal pay, as Harini describes, there still remain real impediments to women receiving genuine equal pay to men for equal work. But in the meantime, as this book explains, the Equality Act 2010 (Gender Pay Gap Information) Regulations 2017 are indeed an important step forward. This book is an invaluable guide to how they work in practice – and indeed how they should be deployed to achieve *best* practice.

I commend the book to you. You will enjoy Harini's views on the inadequacies of the legislation and the regulations and be assisted by her masterly analysis of their provisions.

Elizabeth Gloster
One Essex Court
The Temple
March 2019

PREFACE

Never ask a woman's age,
Never ask a man's wage
– Traditional English proverb

When I was growing up, my mother, an erudite first-generation immigrant doctor, who avidly studied popular and highbrow English culture, and desperately wanted her children to be accepted as British, taught me all the traditional English proverbs. One of those sayings was, "Never ask a woman's age, never ask a man's wage." The message of the proverb – apart from the importance in English culture of suppressing the curiosity which erupts so naturally in Indian culture – is that a woman's value lies in her youthful looks and fertility, and a man's value lies in the money which he earns from paid work.

The key message of this book is that times have changed. I deliberately avoided teaching my own children that particular proverb, because I regard it as sexist, ageist and obsolete. In my opinion, a man has far more to offer the world than the money which he earns from paid work and a woman has far more to offer the world than her youthful looks and fertility; conversely, the money which a woman earns from paid work, and a man's youthful looks and fertility, have their own value and meaning in romantic relationships, families, and the labour market.

In legal terms, the Equality Act 2010 (Gender Pay Gap Information) Regulations 2017 have now struck down the second limb of the proverb. The wages which men earn, compared to their female colleagues, are today very much matters for transparent discussion and scrutiny.

As the country starts to ask openly about a man's wage, follow-on questions of course arise from, "How much does he get paid?". What does he do to earn that sum? What do his colleagues earn? How did he get that job? What is the difference between a workplace where there is unequal pay between men and women and a workplace which has a gender pay gap? If an employer has a gender pay gap, does it mean that the women working there are getting underpaid? If an employer has a gender pay gap, does it mean that women are not getting equal opportunities to enter or progress within its workforce? How can you tell whether an organisation is reporting its gender pay gap information properly? What are the legal risks of not complying with the gender pay gap reporting regime? What are the commercial and reputational risks of not complying with the gender pay gap reporting regime? Why and how should an employer move beyond compliance to best practice in closing its gender pay gap?

In this book, I set out to answer these and other related questions comprehensively, directly, and practically. As a barrister and working woman who has specialised for 20 years in employment and equality law, who is also a company director and a political activist, I have tried my best to write a book which will be useful and readable not only for qualified practising lawyers, such as solicitors in private practice, in-house solicitors, general counsel and barristers, but also for human resources directors, payroll staff, executive officers of companies, non-executive board directors, auditors, workers, and young people planning their careers, who aspire to understand the gender pay gap inside their own organisations and across the British labour market.

To the best of my knowledge and belief, the law and facts quoted in this book are accurate as at 1 March 2019,

Harini Iyengar
London
March 2019
Twitter: @harini_iyengar

ACKNOWLEDGEMENTS

My three children.

Fenella Greenfield, Charlotta Groth, Celia Pilkington.

Liz Gloster.

Tom Evans and Anna Ardanaz-Badia of the Office for National Statistics.

Anthony Horrigan of PayGaps.com.

Tori Rees of GoCompare.

My lay clients, from commerce, the public sector, trade unions and employees, whose individual narratives have cumulatively shaped my understanding of the British labour market and the way in which equal pay law is currently implemented and enforced in practice.

The members of the Temple Women's Forum, the Women's Equality Party, CityParents, Women on Boards, the General Council of the Bar Retention Panel of the Equality Diversity and Social Mobility Committee, and all the parents at the nursery and school gates, who candidly shared their workplace experiences with me.

CONTENTS

CHAPTER ONE
INTRODUCTION

Summary: In this chapter, I provide an overview of the contents of the book, consider the gender pay gap in the United Kingdom, and explain why I welcome the Equality Act 2010 (Gender Pay Gap Information) Regulations 2017 (SI 2017/172) ("the Regulations").

An Overview of the Contents of the Book

This book takes the principle that men and women are entitled to earn equal pay for equal work as well settled in law and in morality. It is therefore fundamentally a book about the enforcement of equal pay law, because the Regulations are the latest enforcement strategy for equal pay law in Great Britain (England, Scotland and Wales).

The most important aim of this book is to explain how employers should comply with the Regulations. I will also consider the cultural, moral and legal origins of equal pay rules, the Equal Pay Act 1970, the equality of terms provisions in the Equality Act 2010, the role of the Equality and Human Rights Commission ("the EHRC") and best practice in closing the gender pay gap. The discussion will cover the complex relationship between the gender pay gap and unequal pay, and explain how and why an employer may decide to conduct a comprehensive equal pay audit instead of simply jumping through the legal hoops required by the Regulations.

The Gender Pay Gap in the United Kingdom

It takes a very long time to change dominant social attitudes and cultures which affect working people and to bring about practical enforcement of new laws. For example, nearly 250 years after *Somersett's*

Case[1] held that chattel slavery was unlawful according to both the common law and statutory rules, so that no one could be forcibly removed from Britain into slavery, the Modern Slavery Act 2015 is still very much relevant and required in order to protect people against labour exploitation.

The gender pay gap is a far subtler form of labour exploitation and inequality than slavery. Yet, it affects much greater numbers of workers in the United Kingdom ("the UK") than modern slavery and it has far bigger economic significance. There are many different ways to break down, measure and then analyse men's pay compared to women's pay.

In this chapter, for simplicity, I adopt the traditional focus of the Office for National Statistics ("the ONS"), which is the difference between median average hourly earnings. It should be noted that the ONS average hourly earnings figures exclude overtime, which is performed far more by men than women workers, mainly because women in the UK still perform the lion's share of childcare and domestic work, compared to men. In fact, women in the UK do more than double the hours of unpaid work, such as childcare, caring for older or disabled adults, cooking, cleaning, laundry and housework than men do[2]. Therefore, the actual difference between men and women employees' take-home pay in the UK is generally speaking considerably wider than the ONS gender pay gap figures indicate, apart from in the most senior and highly-skilled roles, in which the employee is typically required to work whatever hours are necessary to complete the tasks expected, without any entitlement to overtime pay.

The ONS data contains a wealth of current and historic information about the British labour market. It has the advantage of forming a long-

1 Somerset v Stewart (1772) 98 ER 499

2 Office for National Statistics, "Women shoulder the responsibility of 'unpaid work'", 10 November 2016, https://www.ons.gov.uk/employmentandlabourmarket/peopleinwork/earningsandworkinghours/articles/womenshouldertheresponsibilityofunpaidwork/2016-11-10

term research database, using consistent methodology, which reveals trends in the labour market over many years.

On the other hand, I consider that the questions asked in the ONS Annual Survey of Hours and Earnings ("ASHE") have become outdated and out of step with changes in the labour market. The ASHE questions still reflect a bygone post-war era, in which most workers were male breadwinners who did not have any domestic or caring responsibilities in their lives. Typically, it remains the task of payroll staff to supply the ASHE data to the ONS, using the employer's pay records, which traditionally have not captured any further personal data about employees beyond their sex. In the field of equalities law and policy, more and more analysts are adopting an intersectional approach, which in the context of gender pay gaps in the labour market would require acknowledgment and consideration of gender pay gaps between, as a minimum, all the groups with legally-protected characteristics. The ASHE data cannot support an intersectional approach. For example, the ASHE data does not allow employers to see or understand any trends associated with parenthood, age of first and last childbirth, and race in the labour market. If policy-makers, employers and workers wish to close the gender pay gap with an evidence-based strategy, then it is important to establish a way to collect and make available the intersectional data which ASHE cannot provide.

Gender pay gap for median gross hourly earnings (excluding overtime) by age group, UK, April 2018

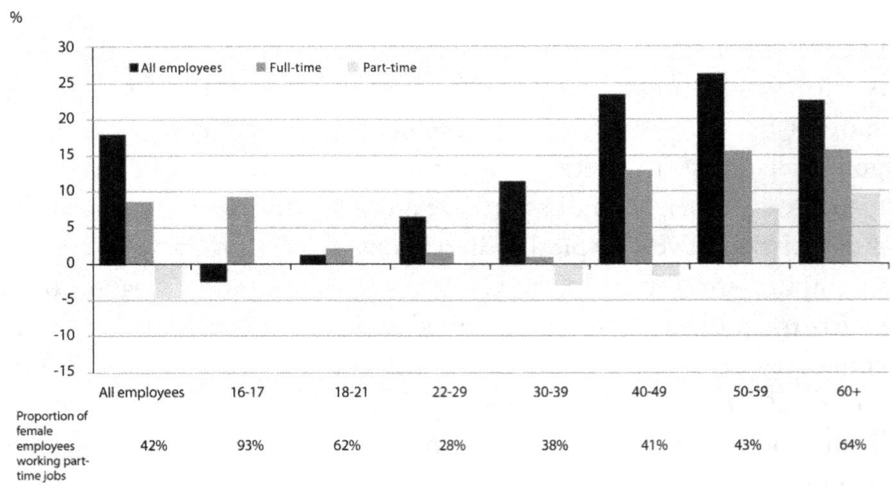

Source: Annual Survey of Hours and Earnings (ASHE) - Office for National Statistics

The most recent ASHE data, for April 2018, published on 25 October 2018[3], shows that amongst full-time employees of all ages, the gender pay gap stands at 8.6%. For full-time employees, the gender pay gap is close to nil for workers aged 18-39, and widens after the age of 40, peaking at a gap over 25% for ages 50-59, when many skilled male workers are at the pinnacle of their careers. Over time, the gender pay gap has narrowed for all age groups since 1997, apart from those aged 60 years and over, for whom it has widened. London, the UK's capital city, is the region with the biggest average gender pay gap between full-time workers, a gap which has barely changed over the last 20 years[4].

---

3 Office for National Statistics, Roger Smith, "Gender pay gap in the UK: 2018", 25 October 2018, https://www.ons.gov.uk/employmentandlabourmarket/peopleinwork/earningsandworkinghours/bulletins/genderpaygapintheuk/2018

4 Office for National Statistics, "London had the smallest gender pay gap 20 years ago, but now it has the largest", 27 November 2017, https://www.ons.gov.uk/employmentandlabourmarket/peopleinwork/earningsandworkinghours/articles/londonhadthesmallestgenderpaygap20yearsagobutnowithasthelargest/2017-11-27

Amongst all employees in the British labour market, both full-time and part-time, the gender pay gap is wider than when only full-time employees are compared. It currently stands at 17.9%. According to the ONS, the higher gender pay gap amongst all employees arises from more women working in part-time jobs, which are lower-paid, with an average hourly rate of £9.36, compared to £14.31 for full-time workers.

Across all employees and across full-time employees, there is only one age at which there is a negative gender pay gap. At ages 16-17, there is a small gender pay gap in favour of teenage girls, of less than 3%, however, taking all teenagers of the same age group who have full-time jobs, there is a gender pay gap in favour of the teenage boys of nearly 10%.

Out of all female employees, 42% work part-time hours. From a peak of 93% at ages 16-17, the proportion of female employees working part-time then drops to 28% between ages 22-29. The percentage of working women who work part-time then rises throughout the age groups, until, amongst the over-60s, 64% of female employees work part-time.

Women dominate the part-time labour force. Across all part-time employees, there is a small negative gender pay gap of less than 5% in favour of women. In other words, women who work part-time tend to earn slightly more than men who work part-time, in terms of hourly pay excluding over-time. Similarly, between ages 30-49, when the gender pay gap for all employees is climbing to its peak of over 25% at ages 50-59, there is a small negative gender pay gap of less than 5% in favour of women who work part-time.

The ONS defines occupations by the Standard Occupational Classific-ation 2010. The ONS website now contains an interactive chart into which full-time and part-time employees can put their occupation and see the gender pay gap[5].

The British labour market remains heavily segregated according to gender[6]. Occupational segregation is a term used to describe a prevalent phenomenon, in which men tend to be over-represented in certain jobs which are stereotypically regarded as suitable for males and which tend to be higher-paid, such as refuse collection truck driver, or data manager or surgeon, whereas women tend to be over-represented in certain jobs which are stereotypically regarded as suitable for females and which tend to be lower-paid, such as school lunchtime meals assistant, librarian or nurse. Vertical stratification describes another widespread phenomenon in the British labour market, in which women tend to be over-represented in the junior and lower-paid levels of the organisational hierarchy, in roles such as classroom teacher, lecturer or junior associate and men tend to be over-represented in the senior and highest-paid levels of the organisational hierarchy, in roles such as headteacher, professor or chief executive officer. The quartile banding within the Regulations provides a crude way for an organisation to begin examining vertical stratification, however, such broad bands will not necessarily throw light on occupational segregation within the workforce, save to the extent that the women are concentrated in the lowest-paid roles. While occupational segregation may not worsen the gender pay gap at lower or more junior levels within an organisation, it is likely to restrict women's opportunities for job progression over time into higher-paid roles.

---

5 Office for National Statistics, "Explore the gender pay gap and test your knowledge", 26 October 2017, https://www.ons.gov.uk/employmentandlabourmarket/peopleinwork/earningsandworkinghours/articles/explorethegenderpaygapandtestyourknowledge/2017-10-26#interactive

6 Office for National Statistics, Jamie Jenkins, "Women in the Labour Market: 2013", 25 September 2013, https://www.ons.gov.uk/employmentandlabourmarket/peopleinwork/employmentandemployeetypes/articles/womeninthelabourmarket/2013-09-25

The gender pay gap is widest in skilled trades occupations

Figure 4: Gender pay gap for median full-time hourly earnings (excluding overtime) and the year-on-year percentage points change, by major occupation group, UK, April 2018

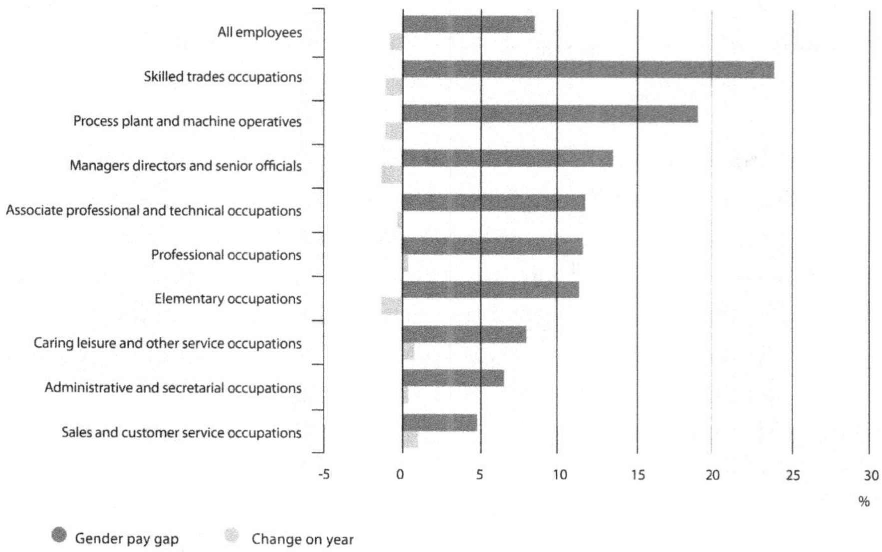

Source: Annual Survey of Hours and Earnings (ASHE) – Office for National Statistics

Broadly speaking, in jobs which are stereotypically regarded in mainstream culture as "women's work", the gender pay gap is narrowest, and in jobs which are stereotypically regarded as "man's work", the gender pay gap is widest. Thus, whilst the gender pay gap amongst full-time employees is in favour of men in all the main occupation groups, it ranges from 4.8% in sales and customer service occupations (stereotypically regarded as more suited to females because of the requirement for good interpersonal skills) to 23.9% in skilled trades and occupations (stereotypically regarded as jobs for working-class men). In professional occupations, the gender pay gap is around 12%, however, it varies widely for different age groups and occupations. For example, in financial services, which has one of the widest gender pay gaps, and which also has many more employees working at a junior level than at senior positions within its hierarchies, and more men than women in senior roles, the gender pay gap is around 55%[7] and for the highest earners, who make £1million or more each year, the gender pay gap is 91%[8].

At the other end of the spectrum of earnings, women in the public sector, and women of colour[9], tend to be concentrated in the lowest-paid jobs, such as cooks, cleaners and care workers. The ASHE does not collect data on gender pay gaps associated with race.

Nor does the ASHE collect data about the gender pay gap which affects disabled women. The British Labour Force Survey 1997-2014 collected some data on disability, using terminology which would now be considered outdated, and which could not be compared to the figures on the gender pay gap and the ethnicity pay gap because of the different historic research methodologies. Despite these shortcomings, the EHRC was able to use the data to predict pay gaps, as between non-disabled male employees and disabled male employees, and as between non-disabled female employees and disabled female employees[10]. For example, the pay gap between the median wage per hour of a non-disabled woman and a woman with a work-limiting and activity-limiting physical disability was 14%. Despite the lack of comprehensive research

7 Haroon Siddique, "City's 'shocking' gender pay gap revealed in equality report," The Guardian, 9 April 2009 reporting on Equality and Human Rights Commission report: https://www.equalityhumanrights.com/en/publication-download/research-report-14-pay-gaps-across-equality-strands (1 April 2009).

8 Caitlin Morrison, "Gender pay gap hits 91% for financial services workers earning more than £1m a year", The Independent, 13 May 2018, https://www.independent.co.uk/news/business/news/gender-pay-gap-men-women-salary-financial-services-one-million-pounds-salary-a8347141.html reporting research by Fox & Partners LLP

9 Fawcett Society, Antony Breach and Yaojun Li, "Gender Pay Gap by Ethnicity in Britain – Briefing", March 2017, https://www.fawcettsociety.org.uk/Handlers/Download.ashx?IDMF=f31d6adc-9e0e-4bfe-a3df-3e85605ee4a9

10 Equality and Human Rights Commission, "Disability: what does the pay gap look like?", 15 August 2017, https://www.equalityhumanrights.com/en/pay-gaps/disability-what-does-pay-gap-look

into the disability gender pay gap, it is obvious that the gender pay gap between disabled female employees and non-disabled male employees is likely to be even wider that the gender pay gap between non-disabled female employees and non-disabled male employees, because of the many structural barriers to disabled women's participation in the labour market[11].

On 30 August 2018, the EHRC called for mandatory reporting by employers of ethnicity and disability pay gaps[12]. The Government started a consultation into ethnicity pay gap reporting[13] on 11 October 2018, which was held in order to inform future policy, and which sought views on what ethnicity pay gap information should be reported by employers to allow for meaningful action, who should be expected to report, and the next steps. The consultation closed on 11 January 2019.

At present, the Government has disclosed no plans to investigate pay gaps created by any other legally-protected characteristics under the Equality Act 2010 (age, disability, gender reassignment, marriage and civil partnership, pregnancy and maternity, religion or belief, or sexual orientation) or by socio-economic origins.

The Regulations focus solely on gender equality. Therefore, the Regulations do not foster an intersectional approach, capable of

11 Papworth Trust, "Facts and Figures: Disability in the UK 2018", Papworth Trust, 2018, https://www.papworthtrust.org.uk/about-us/publications/papworth-trust-disability-facts-and-figures-2018.pdf and Equality and Human Rights Commission, "The Disability Pay Gap", August 2017, https://www.equalityhumanrights.com/sites/default/files/research-report-107-the-disability-pay-gap.pdf

12 Equality and Human Rights Commission, "Data deficit hampering progression of ethnic minority and disabled staff at work", 30 August 2018, https://www.equalityhumanrights.com/en/our-work/news/data-deficit-hampering-progression-ethnic-minority-and-disabled-staff-work

13 Department for Business, Energy and Industrial Strategy, "Ethnicity Pay Reporting: Government Consultation", October 2018, https://assets.publishing.service.gov.uk/government/uploads/system/uploads/attachment_data/file/747546/ethnicity-pay-reporting-consultation.pdf

acknowledging the intersections of privilege and disadvantage in real women's lives.

Why I Welcome the Regulations

Current trends show that it will take around 55 years to close the gender pay gap[14] in Britain (for the "average" woman, ignoring other intersections of inequality which women workers face). This time period is better than the 100 years estimated to close the global gender pay gap internationally[15], however, if we waited 55 years, which is longer than most people's working lives, even my youngest child would probably be a middle-aged grandparent, and I would most probably be dead. It is clear to me that without a concerted and logical strategic plan to enforce equal pay rights for women workers in Britain, an acceptable rate of progress will not be made. Therefore, despite their shortcomings, I welcome the Equality Act 2010 (Gender Pay Gap Information) Regulations 2017 and commend them to you as a potential catalyst for progress. I hope to show you why the Regulations are important and how their impact can be made useful, informative and, ultimately, beneficial, to you and your organisation.

14 Trades Union Congress, Frances O'Grady, " 'Negligible' decrease in gender pay gap is nothing to celebrate, warns TUC," 25 October 2018, https://www.tuc.org.uk/news/%E2%80%9Cnegligible%E2%80%9D-decrease-gender-pay-gap-nothing-celebrate-warns-tuc commenting on Office for National Statistics, Roger Smith, "Gender pay gap in the UK: 2018", 25 October 2018, https://www.ons.gov.uk/employmentandlabourmarket/peopleinwork/earningsandworkinghours/bulletins/genderpaygapintheuk/2018

15 World Economic Forum, "Insight Report: The Global Gender Gap Report 2017", 2017 http://www3.weforum.org/docs/WEF_GGGR_2017.pdf

CHAPTER TWO
THE CULTURAL AND MORAL ORIGINS OF EQUAL PAY FOR EQUAL WORK

Summary: In this chapter, I explain why I take the principle that men and women are entitled to earn equal pay for equal work as well settled in law and in morality, how unequal pay is a means of social control and domination, and the important differences between unequal pay and the gender pay gap.

Why Should Men and Women Get Equal Pay for Equal Work?

In Britain, the idea that people should be paid equal pay for equal work is a recent and radical belief. Throughout ancient and modern British history, many workers have not been accorded the dignity of labour, let alone fair pay or equal pay. In fact, many workers were not accorded personhood or humanity. The use of slavery – whether lawfully used by aristocratic landowners in ancient times or unlawfully used by organised crime syndicates in current times – has been a classic method of political control and domination, despite chattel slavery never being expressly authorised in Britain by statute.

In practice, workers on British soil have historically included chattel slaves treated as items of property owned by their master and bought and sold for money. It is widely believed that slavery existed in pre-Roman Britain. Whether or not it was so, indisputable evidence exists of slavery in Britain from the time of the Roman conquest in 43 AD. Indeed, the Roman Empire and economy were built on slave labour, which was considered a normal part of the social order.

Like the Romans, the Norman invaders of Britain in 1066 cemented their power by taking control of land and slaves. For centuries, under the feudal system, most agricultural workers were serfs or villein, with no right to choose their employer, place of work or type of work, who were compelled to labour for the local lord of the manor. Their duties may even have included serving as soldiers in wartime, whenever called up by the lord. At the time, it was widely believed that such a social hierarchy had been ordained by God, and at the summit was the King, who ruled by divine right.

Following the epidemic of bubonic plague known as the Black Death, which reached Britain in 1348-1350, one third of the population died and the country faced a crisis in the labour market. One of the demands of the unsuccessful Peasants' Revolt in 1381 was an end to serfdom. After the execution of the rebel leaders, the Statute of Cambridge 1388, under which the villein had no freedom of movement away from the place in which they were required to live and work, reinforced restrictions on labourers and shored up the feudal system. It is believed that serfdom gradually declined over the next few centuries, as more and more lords found it advantageous to sell freedom to their serfs in exchange for money.

In more recent centuries, workers in Britain were sold as property in the Trans-Atlantic slave trade, resident in Britain most often as domestic slaves, but most commonly in transit through British ports as agricultural workers to the Caribbean. The experience of West African and Caribbean slaves still forms the contemporary paradigm in the popular imagination and the media of what it means to be enslaved. It is undisputed that the British economy, through slave traders' spending as a new class of nouveau riche, the sponsorship of public works, and financial gains to middle class investors, profited greatly from the unpaid labours of black chattel slaves. Yet, according to the prevalent social attitudes in those days, the Trans-Atlantic slave trade was an acceptable occupation for many men who became wealthy and influential public figures, and also an acceptable form of investment for others.

Meanwhile, despite serfdom falling into disuse, another class of workers, both indigenous Britons and many workers who were trafficked between British colonies, were described as indentured servants or bonded labourers. For them, legal contracts, debts or financial obligations were relied on to explain their lack of freedom over for whom they worked, what work they did, the conditions of that work, the duration of the work (usually several years), and their failure to earn any pay. At the time, however, indentured servants and bonded labourers were not commonly considered to be in the class subjected to slavery.

The next major jolt to the British system of political power and control came with the Industrial Revolution, which began around 1760 with the move from an economy dominated by agriculture towards an economy based in manufacturing, and from handicraft to mechanised production. Over the next century, the British labour force was transformed from a mainly agricultural and scattered countryside workforce into a largely urbanised population concentrated in rapidly-growing towns and cities and working in factories. Mechanisation would eventually have enormous and significant implications for redundancy of the workers employed on the most physical manual labouring tasks. It can be argued that the Industrial Revolution ended the economic model in which keeping a large workforce of slaves, or having a large number of children, was profitable.

In 1772 in *Somersett's Case*[1] it was declared that, having never been made lawful by statute, chattel slavery was also contrary to English common law. Only in 1807, however, was the Slave Trade Act passed, banning slave trading in British colonies.

Meanwhile, another class of impoverished British people were forced to labour under what is now regarded as "workhouse slavery". People who had been unable to find employment, or who were prevented from working by sickness, disability or age, were placed under various social and financial pressures to enter workhouses, where, in exchange for

1 Somerset v Stewart (1772) 98 ER 499

board and lodging, and sometimes access to medical care and schooling, they and their families were compelled to undertake unpaid labour. At the time, workhouses were presented as a socially-responsible way of helping the poor, and were not associated in people's minds with slavery.

As the Industrial Revolution took hold of the British labour market, bitter arguments raged about the economic and political freedom which the new factory workers were acquiring. The Combination Acts 1799 and 1800, which restricted workers' ability to assemble and form unions, were repealed in 1824, only for the Combinations of Workmen Act 1825 to be enacted almost immediately. Under the dominant cultural norms operating in that era, workers' assemblies and trade unions were considered subversive and were banned.

The reference to "Workmen" was no misnomer. Women's work both inside and outside the home was routinely unpaid and, if paid, it was uncontroversially paid at a lower rate to men doing the same jobs[2]. When the right to vote was finally extended to 15-20% of adult males by the Representation of the People Act 1832, to those men who could show that they owned the requisite property, many men living in the sprouting industrial cities were enfranchised, however, no women were entitled to vote.

Eventually, in 1834, the Slavery Abolition Act 1833 became law. Its passage brought a massive transfer of wealth from the country into the pockets of slave owners in compensation, with no financial settlement, property rights or offers of paid employment awarded to the labourers who were freed. Yet, this legal change was widely perceived as a liberal and progressive way to end the Trans-Atlantic slave trade.

2 See, for example, Pat Hudson, "Women's Work", BBC, 29 March 2011, https://www.bbc.co.uk/history/british/victorians/womens_work_01.shtml and Mairead Enright, "Birmingham Women and the Factory Acts", University of Birmingham, 21 March 2018, https://blog.bham.ac.uk/legalherstory/2018/03/21/birmingham-women-and-the-factory-acts/

Until the Married Women's Property Act 1870, any wage which a woman in England earned automatically became her husband's property, through the ancient common law doctrine of coverture. Thus, societal values were far removed from the concept that a woman might earn her own wage and should be paid equally to a male colleague.

Only with the Trade Union Act 1871 did it become lawful for workers to form a trade union. Whilst some women were at the forefront of the burgeoning labour movement, for example, the instigators of the Matchwomen's Strike of 1888, it is important to remember that throughout this period, up to 85% of men and 100% of women had no vote. In those times, it was unthinkable that any legislation requiring pay equality between men and women could appear on the Parliamentary agenda, not least because all the Members of Parliament were men, mostly aristocratic gentlemen who had never depended on a wage.

Finally, with the passage of the Representation of the People Act 1918 and the Parliament (Qualification of Women) Act 1918, women over thirty who could meet the property qualification gained the franchise and the right to stand for Parliament. At the same date, all men were granted the vote whether or not they held property. The right to vote was extended to all women over 21 years of age, regardless of their property ownership, in 1928.

One hundred years after married British women had become legally entitled to hold their own wages, the Equal Pay Act 1970 was passed. The Sex Discrimination Act 1975 came into force on 12 November 1975. Women in the UK first received the right to equal pay for equal work, however, only on 29 December 1975, when the Equal Pay Act 1970 came into force.

In considering the persistence of the pay gap between men and women in Britain, it is important to acknowledge that the idea that men and women should be paid equally for equal work is a relatively new concept in British history, only possible after a series of seismic cultural and legal shifts led to the recognition that women workers were human beings with legal rights.

Unequal Pay is a Means of Control and Domination

Unequal pay is still a means of social control and domination. Today, Britain needs laws against "modern slavery", which was most recently defined and prohibited in the Modern Slavery Act 2015, which often involves human trafficking and the movement of workers around the country, from other countries and from other continents. In the popular imagination, human trafficking is often regarded as synonymous with sex trafficking of prostituted women and children, however, it affects a very wide range of workers, including people kept in agricultural work slavery, or domestic servitude. With contemporary insight into what constitutes the criminal offence of coercive control[3] developing, the category of domestic servitude in present day Britain is wider than many people are prepared to acknowledge.

In contemporary Britain, it is rare to find a director of a business or public body who will confess in front of the media to holding a principled objection to the ideal that in their workforce men and women should receive equal pay for equal work. Nevertheless, any experienced human resources director, recruiter or employment lawyer knows that longstanding British cultural archetypes and stereotypes based on men's and women's respective physical and mental capabilities and aptitudes to perform different types of work remain persistent and widespread. These old-fashioned opinions remain potent, even though they are rarely voiced openly in public settings. Even now, most debates on equal pay – whether popular debates in the mass media or rarified arguments in the specialist Employment Tribunal – revolve around disputes concerning the nature of men's and women's job performance, attitude and ambition, as sex classes, gender identities, and as individual workers.

---

3 Serious Crime Act 2015, section 76

Some people, who favour the legal and political theory of philosophers like John Rawls[4], believe that the existence of the gender pay gap is wrong as a matter of social justice and equality. Other people, who favour the law and economics theory of philosophers like Richard Posner[5], see the gender pay gap as evidence of inefficiency in the operation of the labour market. The Government Equalities Office ("the GEO") uses the language of "fully capitalising on the talent and experience of women"[6].

The Important Differences between Unequal Pay and the Gender Pay Gap

Over four decades after the Equal Pay Act 1970 came into effect, there remains a significant discrepancy between the wages which men earn and the wages which women earn. It is currently fashionable to call this phenomenon the "gender pay gap" and to use that term to describe both unequal pay which is paid in breach of the equal pay or sex discrimination laws and pay differences which do not breach those laws. Therefore, it is vital for people who need to understand the Regulations to understand the conceptual differences between unequal pay caused by unlawful pay structures (ie where women receive lower pay than men for equal work) or by unlawful sex discrimination (ie where conscious or subconscious sexism puts men into the higher-value jobs), and the kind of gender pay gap which is caused either by subtler structural social inequalities, or by legally-justified indirect sex discrimination, both of which are regarded as lawful in Britain.

---

4 John Rawls, "A Theory of Justice", Oxford University Press, 1972

5 Richard Posner, "Economic Analysis of Law", Boston: Little, Brown & Company, 1973

6 See, for example, "Government Response", 17 January 2017, Appendix to "Gender Pay Gap", Women and Equalities Committee's Second Report of Session 2015- 2016, HC 584, 22 March 2016, https://publications.parliament.uk/pa/cm201617/cmselect/cmwomeq/963/96302.htm#footnote-016

In real life, however, the unlawful and lawful causes of individual women colleagues earning less than individual male colleagues in a particular workplace tend to co-exist, overlap and intertwine in complex ways. Therefore, in the future, powerful arguments could be developed that the split in UK law between the lawful and unlawful causes of the differences between men's and women's pay – a split based on a dichotomy between formal legal equality and substantive equality of outcome – conflicts with important norms of international human rights law[7].

The gender pay gap has ignited the imagination and interest of the media in a way which unequal pay never did, and the introduction of mandatory gender pay gap reporting has added fuel to the fire. The detail may seem tedious and statistical, or even arithmetical, however, pay transparency is proving to be a radical stimulus for both the enforcement of existing equal pay law and the widespread review of recruitment and promotion practices across the labour market.

It is clear to me that without a concerted and logical plan properly to enforce the rights originally granted by the Equal Pay Act 1970 to women workers in Britain, equal pay for women and men will not be achieved in our lifetimes. Therefore, despite their shortcomings, I welcome the Equality Act 2010 (Gender Pay Gap Information) Regulations 2017 as an important step forward, and I commend them to you.

---

7 For the view that international human rights law requires states to secure not merely formal legal equality for women but substantive gender equality, see Professor Kathleen Lahey, writing in the context of taxation: "Gender, Taxation, and Equality in Developing Countries" (UNWomen, 2018); "Feminist Judging for Substantive Gender Equality in Tax Law: Changing International and Comparative Constitutional Contexts" in "Feminist Judgments: Rewritten Tax Opinions", ed. Brigitte J. Crawford and Anthony C. Infanti (Cambridge University Press, 2017) 222-52; "Gender Equality and Taxation in Vietnam" (UNWomen 2016, with Pham Thu Hien)

CHAPTER THREE
THE LEGAL ORIGINS OF EQUAL PAY FOR EQUAL WORK

Summary: I shall explain in this chapter the legal origins of the Equal Pay Act 1970, with a broad overview of international equal pay norms.

The International Labour Organization

Despite lacking the capacity to vote or stand for Parliament, British women were very active legal and political campaigners internationally for equality, in the period from the Married Women's Property Act 1870, throughout the First World War, in which Britain participated from 1914 to 1918, until the Representation of the People Act 1918 and the Parliament (Qualification of Women) Act 1918[1]. The International Labour Organization was established in 1919 as part of the Treaty of Versailles, which ended the First World War. The International Labour Organization recognised in the Preamble to its Constitution the principle of equal remuneration for work of equal value[2]. In the inter-war period, women continued to make a vital contribution to the work of the International Labour Organization[3].

---

1 See, for example, Celia Pilkington and Harini Iyengar, "An alternative First World War hero: With commemorations of the First World War under way it seems fitting to remember a remarkable pacifist, barrister and feminist, Chrystal Macmillan", Counsel, December 2014, https://www.counselmagazine.co.uk/articles/alternative-first-world-war-hero; and Carys Lewis, "The archive of the Women's International League for Peace and Freedom (WILPF)", LSE, 30 May 2018, https://blogs.lse.ac.uk/lsehistory/2018/05/30/the-archive-of-the-womens-international-league-for-peace-and-freedom-wilpf/

2 International Labour Organization, "Constitution", 1919, https://www.ilo.org/dyn/normlex/en/f?p=1000:62:0::NO:62:P62_LIST_ENTRIE_ID:2453907:NO

The Universal Declaration of Human Rights

In the aftermath of the Second World War, in which Britain fought from 1939 to 1945, the UK became one of 51 founding members of the United Nations on 24 October 1945, and a permanent member of the UN Security Council. The Universal Declaration of Human Rights ("the UDHR") was adopted by the United Nations General Assembly on 10 December 1948. Article 23 provides[4]:

> 1. Everyone has the right to work, to free choice of employment, to just and favourable conditions of work and to protection against unemployment.
> 2. Everyone, without any discrimination, has the right to equal pay for equal work.
> 3. Everyone who works has the right to just and favourable remuneration ensuring for himself and his family an existence worthy of human dignity, and supplemented, if necessary, by other means of social protection.
> 4. Everyone has the right to form and to join trade unions for the protection of his interests.

It is notable that the UDHR does not treat unequal pay because of sex separately from unequal pay because of any other form of discrimination. Further, the UDHR does not separate everyone's right to earn just and favourable remuneration from the right to receive other means of social protection which enable her to provide for herself and her family an existence worthy of human dignity.

---

3 International Labour Office, "Women's empowerment: 90 years of ILO action!", 2009 (?), https://www.ilo.org/wcmsp5/groups/public/@dgreports/@gender/documents/publication/wcms_105088.pdf

4 The United Nations, "Universal Declaration of Human Rights", 1948, http://www.un.org/en/universal-declaration-human-rights/

The European Convention for the Protection of Human Rights and Fundamental Freedoms

Most of the international human rights norms then evolved into regional norms. The members of the Council of Europe signed the European Convention for the Protection of Human Rights and Fundamental Freedoms ("the ECHR") on 4 November 1950, and the UK was the first signatory. On 8 March 1951, the UK Parliament ratified the ECHR and it came into force on 3 September 1953.

Article 4 of the ECHR prohibits slavery and forced labour and Article 11 protects the right to form and join trade unions, however, the right to equal pay for equal work is not mentioned. The Human Rights Act 1998 incorporated the ECHR into domestic law from 2 October 2000. It is important to remember that the Human Rights Act 1998, like the ECHR, does not provide a right for women workers in the UK to receive equal pay for equal work to men workers.

The Role of European Employment Law

The international human rights norm of equal pay for equal work, including for women, found its way into UK law not through the ECHR but through European employment law. At the time of writing, the UK is on course to leave the European Union on 29 March 2019 without a withdrawal agreement which preserves the many important rights which British women workers acquired through European employment law. Nevertheless, the current Prime Minister, Theresa May, has stated that workers' existing legal rights will be guaranteed during her period in office[5]. Amongst various and conflicting proposals, the Government has also suggested at certain times that the direct effect of relevant rights under European law will persist after the UK quits the European Union and that judgments of the European Court of Justice will be given effect in domestic law at the point of exit. No promises,

5 https://researchbriefings.parliament.uk/ResearchBriefing/Summary/CBP-7732

however, have been made, nor could any promises contained in political speeches or election manifestos be relied on within our current doctrine of Parliamentary sovereignty.

Therefore, for the practical purposes of writing this book, I am compelled to assume that our equal pay laws will remain in their current form for the foreseeable future, and will continue to reflect European employment law. It follows that European employment law at the point of exit will remain relevant to employers and employees in Britain.

The Treaty for the Functioning of the European Union, commonly known as the Treaty of Rome, was signed on 25 March 1957 by Belgium, France, Italy, Luxembourg, the Netherlands and West Germany and came into force on 1 January 1958. Article 157[6] (formerly article 141) creates a duty on each member state to ensure that the principle of equal pay for male and female workers for equal work or work of equal value is applied:

> 1. Each Member State shall ensure that the principle of equal pay for male and female workers for equal work or work of equal value is applied.
>
> 2. For the purpose of this article, 'pay' means the ordinary basic or minimum wage or salary and any other consideration, whether in cash or in kind, which the worker receives directly or indirectly, in respect of his employment, from his employer.
>
> Equal pay without discrimination based on sex means:
>
> (a) that pay for the same work at piece rates shall be calculated on the basis of the same unit of measurement;

---

6 Eur-Lex Access to European Union Law, Document 12016E157, 7 June 2016, https://eur-lex.europa.eu/legal-content/EN/TXT/?uri=CELEX:12016E157

> (b) that pay for work at time rates shall be the same for the same job.
>
> 3. The European Parliament and the Council, acting in accordance with the ordinary legislative procedure, and after consulting the Economic and Social Committee, shall adopt measures to ensure the application of the principle of equal opportunities and equal treatment of men and women in matters of employment and occupation, including the principle of equal pay for equal work or work of equal value.
>
> 4. With a view to ensuring full equality in practice between men and women in working life, the principle of equal treatment shall not prevent any Member State from maintaining or adopting measures providing for specific advantages in order to make it easier for the underrepresented sex to pursue a vocational activity or to prevent or compensate for disadvantages in professional careers.

Following two unsuccessful applications to join the European Union in 1963 and 1967, the UK reapplied successfully and joined on 1 January 1973, a decision which was subsequently endorsed by popular vote in a referendum on 5 June 1975.

Across the European Union, women earn on average 16.2% less than men for each hour worked in terms of gross pay[7]. The difference in the overall average annual earnings between women and men, on the other hand, stands at 39.6%, which takes into account three types of disadvantage which women commonly face: lower hourly earnings, working fewer hours in paid jobs, and lower employment rates, for example, because of career breaks to care for children or relatives.

---

7 European Commission, "The gender pay gap in the European Union", November 2018, https://ec.europa.eu/info/sites/info/files/aid_development_cooperation_fundamental_rights/equalpayday-eu-factsheets-2018_en.pdf

On 7 March 2014, in European Commission Recommendation D(2014) 1405[8], the expectation was set that member states would start tackling the gender pay gap more seriously, by giving employees an entitlement to request information about pay levels in their workplace, by requiring regular reporting by employers on pay levels, and by requiring larger companies to conduct pay audits.

The UK Government was required to report by the end of 2015 on the steps it had taken. Its voluntary scheme for employers to conduct and publish equal pay audits had had only four takers[9], and had patently been ineffective. Similarly, there are no reported examples of an Employment Tribunal ever using its power under the Equality Act 2010 (Equal Pay Audits) Regulations 2014 to order an employer which had lost an equal pay claim to publish an equal pay audit.

The origins of the right to equal pay for equal work lies not in international human rights law but in the law of the European Union. So, the belated implementation of mandatory gender gap reporting through the Regulations might be regarded not as a feminist step forward by a modern Government, so much as the last resort for an administration which had consistently done the bare minimum which it was required to do by European Union rules. Therefore, it is impossible to predict what effect Britain's exit from the European Union might have on gender pay gap reporting and the enforcement of equal pay law in Britain, despite the assumptions which I have made in this chapter.

---

8 Publications Office of the European Union, "Commission Recommendation of 7 March 2014 on strengthening the principle of equal pay between men and women through transparency", 7 March 2014, https://publications.europa.eu/en/publication-detail/-/publication/b8668ea5-a69a-11e3-8438-01aa75ed71a1/language-en

9 Rajeev Syal, "Just four companies reveal gender pay gap under coalition scheme", The Guardian, 12 August 2014, https://www.theguardian.com/money/2014/aug/12/gender-pay-gap-coalition-scheme

CHAPTER FOUR
THE LEGACY OF THE EQUAL PAY ACT 1970

Summary: In this chapter, I will provide essential reading on the eccentric and outdated legal system by which women's right to equal pay is enforced in Great Britain. I consider that the unwieldy and technically complex regime created by the Equal Pay Act 1970 has been a major contributor to the poor practical enforcement of women's right to equal pay and the persistence of the gender pay gap[1].

The Eccentric and Outdated Equal Pay Regime

The equal pay regime in Great Britain (England, Scotland and Wales: equal pay and the gender pay gap in Northern Ireland are beyond the scope of this book) is a legal regime unique and distinct from the rules which govern other kinds of sex discrimination in the workplace. Other kinds of sex discrimination in the workplace, for example, not offering a woman a promotion because of sexist attitudes, or workplace sexual harassment, are characterised as statutory torts, however, failure to pay a woman worker equal pay for equal work is characterised as a breach of an implied contractual term. Despite the use of the word "gender" in the Regulations, the equal pay laws in Britain are based on "the difference of sex" and take a binary view of a person's sex in comparison to a legal comparator of "the opposite sex".

The equal pay rules also stand apart from the rules which govern unequal pay between groups who have and do not have the other legally-protected characteristics (age, disability, gender reassignment, marriage and civil partnership, race, religion or belief and sexual orient-

1 See further Harini Iyengar, "Birmingham City Council v Abdulla (2012)", "Women's Legal Landmarks", Chapter 83, Hart, 2019

ation). If an employee complains to an Employment Tribunal because he believes that he is being unlawfully paid less than a colleague because of his age, disability, gender reassignment, marriage and civil partnership, race, religion or belief, or sexual orientation, he must do so by bringing a direct discrimination claim under section 13[2] of the Equality Act 2010 and to win the claim, he will need to prove that he was paid less than the colleague because of his protected characteristic. In contrast, if a woman employee complains to an Employment Tribunal because she believes that she is being unlawfully paid less than a male colleague for equal work because she is a woman, or because of pregnancy or maternity, she must do so by bringing an equal pay claim under sections 64-80 of the Equality Act 2010, and to win her claim she will need to prove that her employer has breached a fictitious term in her contract of employment which entitled her to receive equal pay for equal work. Someone who brings a discrimination claim that he is paid less than a colleague because he possesses any of the other protected characteristic has to show under section 23 of the Equality Act 2010 simply that there is "no material difference between the circumstances relating to each case" as between himself and the better-paid colleague; a woman with an equal pay claim must satisfy the detailed rules on comparators, associated employers and same establishment set out in sections 79 and 80 of the Equality Act 2010.

It should also be understood at the outset that the equal pay laws in Britain prohibit employers from paying a woman less than a man only when she does "work that is equal to the work" he does. There is no rule of English law requiring employers to provide "fair" pay in relation to the difficulty or working conditions of the job. The National Minimum Wage Regulations 2015 impose minimum hourly rates of pay on employers, and many businesses and public bodies voluntarily follow the pay recommendations of the popular campaign group, the Living Wage Foundation, which are based on the cost of living rather than the statutory requirements.

---

2 In theory, depending on the facts, he may also or alternatively be able to bring a claim of indirect discrimination under section 19 of the Equality Act 2010.

At the heart of Britain's unwieldy and technically-complex equal pay law, and, in my view, the root of the complex procedural and substantive barriers to practical enforcement of the right to equal pay, is the legal fiction of the sex equality clause, which is implied into the contract of employment by automatic operation of law. This legal fiction was created by a male-dominated Parliament in the Equal Pay Act 1970, and transported, almost unchanged in substance although set out more cogently, and updated to reflect caselaw, by another male-dominated Parliament, into the Equality Act 2010.

CHAPTER FIVE
THE EQUALITY OF TERMS PROVISIONS IN THE EQUALITY ACT 2010

Summary: In this chapter, I explain the complex equality of terms provisions in the Equality Act 2010 which provide the right to equal pay for equal work in Britain.

The Equality of Terms Provisions

A failure by an employer to pay equal pay is characterised as a breach of a contractual term which is imposed into all contracts of employment by operation of law and which says that an employer will pay men and women equal pay for equal work. It is a statutory interference by Parliament with the rules of the English common law of contract, whose starting point is that individuals and businesses should have freedom to enter into whatever contracts they would like. Nevertheless, because equal pay operates through the imposition of the equality term, it remains up to each woman whether she chooses to enforce her contractual right to equal pay or not. The Equality Act 2010 does not treat women workers' right to equal pay as a pay issue to be regulated and enforced by the state, for example, as the national minimum wage is regulated and enforced by the state.

The equality of terms provisions in the Equality Act 2010 refer to "person A", and their right to equal pay regardless of their sex, and to a comparator colleague "person B", who is "of the opposite sex", only rarely mentioning "men" and "women". The vast majority of equal pay claims in Britain are made by women, relying on comparators who are men. Therefore, for the sake of simplicity and clarity, in this chapter I shall often refer to "person A" as "the woman" and to "person B" as "the man".

Chapter 3 of the Equality Act 2010 contains the Equality of Terms provisions in relation to sex equality.

Section 64 – Relevant types of work

Section 64 provides:

> 64 Relevant types of work
>
> (1) Sections 66 to 70 apply where—
>
> (a) a person (A) is employed on work that is equal to the work that a comparator of the opposite sex (B) does;
>
> (b) a person (A) holding a personal or public office does work that is equal to the work that a comparator of the opposite sex (B) does.
>
> (2) The references in subsection (1) to the work that B does are not restricted to work done contemporaneously with the work done by A.

Section 64 sets up the essential equal pay paradigm of a woman who is employed to do "work that is equal to the work that a comparator of the opposite sex" does. Women who hold a personal or public office are also protected, however, across the British labour market, very few women workers hold a personal or public office.

To establish her right to equal pay for equal work, the woman worker must at the very outset prove that she is "employed" under section 64(1)(a), which means with the legal status of "employee", in contrast, say, to being truly self-employed in her own right or a "worker" other than an employee. In the modern labour market, with the major shift to new and variable forms of employment status, including substantial increases in questionable self-employment, zero hours contracts, agency working and novel hybrid arrangements[1], the requirement to be "employed" greatly reduces the number of working women who can benefit from the right to equal pay.

The second threshold criterion for her to prove is that the work which she is employed to do is "equal" within the meaning of the law to the work which her male colleague does. With the high level of gender segregation and specialisation in the British labour market[2], the requirement of proving a suitable male comparator within the meaning of the law again narrows down the number of women workers who can benefit from the right to equal pay. Subsection 64(2) allows a woman to rely on work which her male comparator does other than work which they do during the same time period. In other words, she can point to a male comparator who was doing equal work to her either before her own job started, or after it ended. Nevertheless, it is routine these days, in both public sector and private sector workplaces, to see regular reorganisations or workplace roles every few years, often including changes in pay and bonus structures. It is therefore rarely straightforward for a woman to succeed in establishing an equal pay claim based on a male comparator whom she says did "equal work" to her, but who was not employed contemporaneously with her performing that work.

---

1 See, for example, the novel "self-employed plus" status agreed by Hermes and GMB union, BBC, "Hermes in 'ground-breaking' pay deal for couriers", 4 February 2019, https://www.bbc.co.uk/news/business-47110934

2 See, for example, Maya Oppenheim, "Women still face 'massive gender bias' in UK workforce, new AI study finds", Independent, 20 February 2019, reporting research by the Royal Statistical Society that 95% of receptionists, legal secretaries and care assistants are female in the UK, while 85% of investment bankers, 82% of Chief Executive Officers and 73% of directors are male, https://www.independent.co.uk/news/uk/home-news/women-gender-bias-uk-workforce-men-ai-a8786936.html

Section 65 – Equal work

The concept of equal work is defined in section 65. There are three ways in which a woman can prove in legal proceedings that her work was equal to a male comparator's work. The argument that the work of the woman and the man are equal can be based upon "like work", "work rated as equivalent" or "work of equal value", and there is forty years of complex caselaw explaining how those three technical legal definitions from the statute should be interpreted in a range of real-life situations. Section 65 provides:

> 65 Equal work
>
> (1) For the purposes of this Chapter, A's work is equal to that of B if it is—
>
> (a) like B's work,
>
> (b) rated as equivalent to B's work, or
>
> (c) of equal value to B's work.
>
> (2) A's work is like B's work if—
>
> (a) A's work and B's work are the same or broadly similar, and
>
> (b) such differences as there are between their work are not of practical importance in relation to the terms of their work.
>
> (3) So on a comparison of one person's work with another's for the purposes of subsection (2), it is necessary to have regard to—
>
> (a) the frequency with which differences between their work occur in practice, and
>
> (b) the nature and extent of the differences.
>
> (4) A's work is rated as equivalent to B's work if a job evaluation study—
>
> (a) gives an equal value to A's job and B's job in terms of the demands made on a worker, or

(b) would give an equal value to A's job and B's job in those terms were the evaluation not made on a sex-specific system.

(5) A system is sex-specific if, for the purposes of one or more of the demands made on a worker, it sets values for men different from those it sets for women.

(6) A's work is of equal value to B's work if it is—

(a) neither like B's work nor rated as equivalent to B's work, but

(b) nevertheless equal to B's work in terms of the demands made on A by reference to factors such as effort, skill and decision-making.

The first way in which a woman can prove that she is doing equal work to a male colleague is to show that they are both performing "like work". It is "like work" if it is the "same or broadly similar" and whatever differences exist between their work "are not of practical importance in relation to the terms of their work", which means the terms contained in the contracts of employment. Further, when deciding whether they are doing "like work" to each other, the Employment Tribunal or court will pay regard to "the frequency with which differences between their work occur in practice, and the nature and extent of the differences."

The second way is to prove that the comparators are performing "work rated as equivalent" to each other. Under this definition, the woman must show that either a job evaluation study gives an equal value to their jobs in terms of the demands made on them as workers, or a job evaluation study not on a sex-specific system would (supposing you did one) give equal value to their jobs. A job evaluation study is a formal assessment of a job to assess how challenging it is, usually by reference to requirements such as the skill, effort and responsibility, and in the context of equal pay, the objective is to rank different jobs according to how demanding they are compared to one another. The Korn Ferry Hay job evaluation methodology (formerly the Hay job evaluation methodology) is an example of a popular system. Generally speaking, large-scale job evaluation studies have been more common in the public sector than in the private sector. A sex-specific system is one which sets different values for men and women for the purposes of one or more of the demands made on a worker, in other words, a sexist job evaluation methodology. It is therefore possible for a woman to challenge the outcome of a job evaluation study which does not rate her work as equivalent to her male comparator's, if she can establish an argument that the study itself was sex-specific.

The third way in which a woman can prove that her work is equal work is to argue that it is of "equal value". In practice, claims of equal value are often put to the bottom of the list of issues in equal claims, to be dealt with at the very end of the hearings and only if absolutely unavoidable, because of their perceived complexity compared to "like work" or "work rated as equivalent", in terms of both the concepts and the evidence required. For the comparators' work to be of equal value to each other, it must not be "like work" nor "work rated as equivalent", but it must be equal in terms of the demands made on the worker "by reference to factors such as effort, skill and decision-making". The concept of "equal value" tends to start at a very abstract level and then gradually become very concrete as the witnesses come to give evidence in a hearing about the nitty-gritty of exactly what specific tasks they each did at work, for how long, for how long compared to other tasks, and over what time period.

The requirement to prove that the work being done was "equal work" within one of these three complicated definitions is onerous for equal pay claimants. Naturally, given the complexity of the legal definitions, the first line of defence which an employer typically takes in response to an equal pay claim is routinely simply to deny that the man and the women were doing "equal work" at the relevant times. In my view, the question whether the woman and man were doing "equal work" is generally at the crux of whether the employer will be able to defend the claim successfully or whether the woman will win her case. It is typically far harder for an employer to establish a defence to an equal pay claim, in my opinion, than to win at the outset with an effective rebuttal of the woman's assertion that she was doing "equal work" to the man. Many months, if not years, are often spent on the question of "equal work" in equal pay litigation.

Section 66 – Sex equality clause

At the heart of the eccentric mechanism by which the right to equal pay for equal work is protected in law is the fictional "sex equality clause", found in section 66 of the Equality Act 2010:

> Sex equality clause
>
> (1) If the terms of A's work do not (by whatever means) include a sex equality clause, they are to be treated as including one.
>
> (2) A sex equality clause is a provision that has the following effect—
>
> (a) if a term of A's is less favourable to A than a corresponding term of B's is to B, A's term is modified so as not to be less favourable;
>
> (b) if A does not have a term which corresponds to a term of B's that benefits B, A's terms are modified so as to include such a term.
>
> (3) Subsection (2)(a) applies to a term of A's relating to membership of or rights under an occupational pension scheme only in so far as a sex equality rule would have effect in relation to the term.
>
> (4) In the case of work within section 65(1)(b), a reference in subsection (2) above to a term includes a reference to such terms (if any) as have not been determined by the rating of the work (as well as those that have).

Section 66 provides that if the terms of a person's contract of employment do not, by whatever means, include a sex equality clause, then the terms are to be treated by the courts as including a sex equality clause. In other words, section 66 implies by operation of law into every contract of employment in Britain a new clause which the parties did not bargain for. This is a significant exception to the doctrine of freedom of contract, under which parties are at liberty to enter into whatever contracts, terms and conditions they freely choose. It is striking to me that, in twenty years of practice in employment law, I have yet to see an express sex equality clause in any contract of employment, despite the implication by statute of a sex equality clause since 1975. Many employers have Staff Handbooks which refer to equal opportunities in general terms or refer to the statutory provisions on discrimination law, however, I have not come across any Staff Handbook which says explicitly that all employees benefit from a contractual sex equality clause.

The effect of the sex equality clause is explained in section 66(2). Any term in the woman's contract of employment which is less favourable to her than a corresponding term of the man's contract of employment is automatically modified by operation of law, so as to be not less favourable. Similarly, if the man benefits from a term in his contract of employment and she does not have a corresponding term in her contract of employment, the woman's contract of employment is automatically modified by operation of law to include such a term.

Section 67 – Sex equality rule

Section 67 of the Equality Act 2010 imposes the sex equality rule into occupational pension schemes by automatic operation of law:

> 67 Sex equality rule
>
> (1) If an occupational pension scheme does not include a sex equality rule, it is to be treated as including one.
>
> (2) A sex equality rule is a provision that has the following effect —

(a) if a relevant term is less favourable to A than it is to B, the term is modified so as not to be less favourable;

(b) if a term confers a relevant discretion capable of being exercised in a way that would be less favourable to A than to B, the term is modified so as to prevent the exercise of the discretion in that way.

(3) A term is relevant if it is—

(a) a term on which persons become members of the scheme, or

(b) a term on which members of the scheme are treated.

(4) A discretion is relevant if its exercise in relation to the scheme is capable of affecting—

(a) the way in which persons become members of the scheme, or

(b) the way in which members of the scheme are treated.

(5) The reference in subsection (3)(b) to a term on which members of a scheme are treated includes a reference to the term as it has effect for the benefit of dependants of members.

(6) The reference in subsection (4)(b) to the way in which members of a scheme are treated includes a reference to the way in which they are treated as the scheme has effect for the benefit of dependants of members.

(7) If the effect of a relevant matter on a person (A) differs according to the effect it has on a person of the same sex as A, according to whether A is married, in a civil partnership, or for some other reason due to A's family status, a comparison for the purposes of this section of the effect of that matter on persons of the opposite sex must be with a person of the opposite sex to A who is in the same position as A and in particular—

(a) where A is married to someone of the opposite sex, A is to be compared to a person of the opposite sex to A ("B") where B is married to someone of the opposite sex to B;

(b) where A is married to someone of the same sex as A or is in a civil partnership, A is to be compared to B where B is married to someone of the same sex as B or is in a civil partnership.

(8) A relevant matter is—

(a) a relevant term;

(b) a term conferring a relevant discretion;

(c) the exercise of a relevant discretion in relation to an occupational pension scheme.

(9) This section, so far as relating to the terms on which persons become members of an occupational pension scheme, does not have effect in relation to pensionable service before 8 April 1976.

(10) This section, so far as relating to the terms on which members of an occupational pension scheme are treated, does not have effect in relation to pensionable service before 17 May 1990.

Section 68 of the Equality Act 2010 empowers the trustees or managers of an occupational pension scheme to make sex equality alternations to the pension scheme by resolution, which may have retrospective effect over a period of time prior to the date of the resolution:

68 Sex equality rule: consequential alteration of schemes

(1) This section applies if the trustees or managers of an occupational pension scheme do not have power to make sex equality alterations to the scheme.

(2) This section also applies if the trustees or managers of an occupational pension scheme have power to make sex equality alterations to the scheme but the procedure for doing so—

(a) is liable to be unduly complex or protracted, or

(b) involves obtaining consents which cannot be obtained or which can be obtained only with undue delay or difficulty.

(3) The trustees or managers may by resolution make sex equality alterations to the scheme.

(4) Sex equality alterations may have effect in relation to a period before the date on which they are made.

(5) Sex equality alterations to an occupational pension scheme are such alterations to the scheme as may be required to secure conformity with a sex equality rule.

Section 69 – Defence of material factor

The main defence which one sees in equal pay claims is found in section 69 of the Equality Act 2010. Under the Equal Pay Act 1970, the defence could be established where the variation in pay was "genuinely due to a material factor which is not the difference of sex", widely known as "the GMF defence". It is now more accurately known as the "material factor" defence.

The gist of the defence is that the employer argues that the sex equality rule does not apply to the women's pay in this case, because the difference between the woman's and the man's pay is nothing to do with her being a woman, since the reason for the difference in pay is a material factor which does not involve treating the woman less favourably because of her sex than the man is treated and which is a proportionate means of achieving a legitimate aim.

In terms of the overall technical scheme of the Equality Act 2010, including, in particular, the anti-discrimination provisions, a material factor defence can be established where an employer proves that the reason for the difference in pay is not an unjustifiable indirectly sex discriminatory reason. Indirect sex discrimination in the workplace, contrary to section 19 of the Equality Act 2010, arises where the employer applies to the employee a provision, criterion or practice which is discriminatory in relation to sex. A discriminatory provision, criterion or practice is one which the employer applies or would apply to men and women, which puts or would put women to a particular disadvantage compared to men, which puts the individual woman claimant to that disadvantage in real life, and which the employer cannot show to be a proportionate means of achieving a legitimate aim. Section 19 says:

> 19 Indirect discrimination
>
> (1) A person (A) discriminates against another (B) if A applies to B a provision, criterion or practice which is discriminatory in relation to a relevant protected characteristic of B's.
>
> (2) For the purposes of subsection (1), a provision, criterion or practice is discriminatory in relation to a relevant protected characteristic of B's if—
>
> (a) A applies, or would apply, it to persons with whom B does not share the characteristic,
>
> (b) it puts, or would put, persons with whom B shares the characteristic at a particular disadvantage when compared with persons with whom B does not share it,
>
> (c) it puts, or would put, B at that disadvantage, and
>
> (d) A cannot show it to be a proportionate means of achieving a legitimate aim.
>
> (3) The relevant protected characteristics are—
>
> age;
>
> disability;
>
> gender reassignment;
>
> marriage and civil partnership;
>
> race;
>
> religion or belief;
>
> sex;
>
> sexual orientation.

It is significant to note that under section 69(3), the long-term objective of reducing inequality between men's and women's terms of work is always to be regarded as a legitimate aim.

Section 69 provides:

> 69 Defence of material factor
>
> (1) The sex equality clause in A's terms has no effect in relation to a difference between A's terms and B's terms if the responsible person shows that the difference is because of a material factor reliance on which—
>
> (a) does not involve treating A less favourably because of A's sex than the responsible person treats B, and
>
> (b) if the factor is within subsection (2), is a proportionate means of achieving a legitimate aim.
>
> (2) A factor is within this subsection if A shows that, as a result of the factor, A and persons of the same sex doing work equal to A's are put at a particular disadvantage when compared with persons of the opposite sex doing work equal to A's.
>
> (3) For the purposes of subsection (1), the long-term objective of reducing inequality between men's and women's terms of work is always to be regarded as a legitimate aim.
>
> (4) A sex equality rule has no effect in relation to a difference between A and B in the effect of a relevant matter if the trustees or managers of the scheme in question show that the difference is because of a material factor which is not the difference of sex.
>
> (5) "Relevant matter" has the meaning given in section 67.
>
> (6) For the purposes of this section, a factor is not material unless it is a material difference between A's case and B's.

Section 70 – Exclusion of sex discrimination provisions

Just as the Equal Pay Act 1970 used to do, section 70 of the Equality Act 2010 splits jurisdiction between sex discrimination and equal pay. This means that someone who possesses any of the other protected characteristics than sex, pregnancy or maternity may bring a discrimination claim that because of his protected characteristic he was unlawfully paid less than a colleague who lacked that protected characteristic and who did the same work. On the other hand, a woman may not bring a discrimination claim that she was unlawfully paid less than a male colleague who did the same work, because she is a woman or because she was pregnant or had a baby. Her only redress is an equal pay claim:

> 70 Exclusion of sex discrimination provisions
>
> (1) The relevant sex discrimination provision has no effect in relation to a term of A's that—
>
> (a) is modified by, or included by virtue of, a sex equality clause or rule, or
>
> (b) would be so modified or included but for section 69 or Part 2 of Schedule 7.
>
> (2) Neither of the following is sex discrimination for the purposes of the relevant sex discrimination provision—
>
> (a) the inclusion in A's terms of a term that is less favourable as referred to in section 66(2)(a);
>
> (b) the failure to include in A's terms a corresponding term as referred to in section 66(2)(b).
>
> (3) The relevant sex discrimination provision is, in relation to work of a description given in the first column of the table, the provision referred to in the second column so far as relating to sex.

Description of work	Provision
Employment	Section 39(2)
Appointment to a personal office	Section 49(6)
Appointment to a public office	Section 50(6)

Section 71 – Sex discrimination in relation to contractual pay

Section 71 of the Equality Act 2010 contains a new provision, which was not included in the Equal Pay Act 1970. It caters for the situation in which a woman argues that a male colleague who is doing a less demanding job than her is being paid more than her. In other words, she cannot show a male comparator who is doing equal work to herself, and she is arguing that she should have been paid more than her male colleague was paid. Under the Equal Pay Act 1970, women in her situation could not establish their equal pay claims. Now, under section 71 of the Equality Act 2010, a woman can argue this type of equal pay claim as a sex discrimination claim, by relying on evidence which includes the fact that a real-life man doing a less demanding job than her was in fact paid more than her by the employer, to argue that had she been a hypothetical man doing her job, she would have been paid more. Section 71 provides:

> Sex discrimination in relation to contractual pay
>
> (1) This section applies in relation to a term of a person's work—
>
> (a) that relates to pay, but
>
> (b) in relation to which a sex equality clause or rule has no effect.
>
> (2) The relevant sex discrimination provision (as defined by section 70) has no effect in relation to the term except in so far as treatment of the person amounts to a contravention of the provision by virtue of section 13 or 14.

I have not yet come across any caselaw on section 71, but I have successfully pleaded this type of sex discrimination claim, amongst others, in an equal pay claim which settled out of court.

Intellectually, it is very difficult to reach a principled explanation as to why it was considered sensible by legislators to categorise equal pay claims based on section 71 of the Equality Act 2010 as sex discrimination claims, and all equal pay claims based on protected characteristics other than sex, pregnancy or maternity likewise as discrimination claims, but to categorise common or garden sex-based equal pay claims as breach of contract claims justiciable only under the equal pay provisions, which are very complex and slow-moving, both procedurally and substantively.

Section 72 – Relevant types of work

Sections 72 to 76 of the Equality Act 2010 contain very specific provisions on pregnancy and maternity equality and pay.

Under section 72, sections 73 to 76 apply where a woman is employed or holds a personal or public office:

> 72 Relevant types of work
>
> Sections 73 to 76 apply where a woman—
>
> (a) is employed, or
>
> (b) holds a personal or public office.

Section 73 – Maternity equality clause

Section 73 follows the pattern of the fictional sex equality clause implying by automatic operation of law a maternity equality clause into every contract of employment:

73 Maternity equality clause

(1) If the terms of the woman's work do not (by whatever means) include a maternity equality clause, they are to be treated as including one.

(2) A maternity equality clause is a provision that, in relation to the terms of the woman's work, has the effect referred to in section 74(1), (6) and (8).

(3) In the case of a term relating to membership of or rights under an occupational pension scheme, a maternity equality clause has only such effect as a maternity equality rule would have.

Section 74 – Maternity equality clause: pay

Section 74 sets out the conditions under which a term of a woman's contract of employment covering maternity-related pay will be automatically altered by operation of law.

The first effect is to grant a woman who is absent on maternity leave increases in her maternity pay which arise from increases in her salary, from which she would have benefited, had she not been absent on maternity leave. Maternity-related pay is pay to which a woman is entitled because she is pregnant or on maternity leave, but which is not statutory maternity pay. In other words, maternity-related pay is pay which an employer is not obliged by statute to pay her, but which it freely contracts to pay to a woman employee who is pregnant or on maternity leave, presumably in order to make it financially sustainable for her to have children and to increase the prospects that the employer will be able to retain her in its workforce in the long run.

The whole section is drafted on the assumption that the mother's pay whilst on maternity leave will be significantly lower than her normal pay, so that even this small increase, related to a change in her normal pay, is very important to award her. Conversely, if the woman is being paid at her normal rate of pay whilst on maternity leave, then section 74 does not entitle her to any pay rises which she would have received had she been at work and not on maternity leave. As times change, more employers are offering women maternity pay at 100% of their normal salary, including a handful offering up to 26 weeks at full pay[3]. At the time of writing, ahead of the pack was the financial services business, GoCompare, which offered nine months at full pay for mothers and fathers[4].

Section 74 also provides for women to earn bonuses during maternity leave, but, again, in a very restricted way. Her contract will be modified so as to entitle her to receive the bonus pay, but only in respect of the period of time when she was at work prior to starting maternity leave, or the period when she was compulsory maternity leave[5], or the period after she returned to work.

Finally, section 74 makes clear that a mother employee is entitled to receive a pay rise after her return to work after giving birth, if she would have benefited from that pay rise had she not taken maternity leave:

> 74 Maternity equality clause: pay
>
> (1) A term of the woman's work that provides for maternity-related pay to be calculated by reference to her pay at a particular

---

3 Dusty Baxter-Wright, "11 of the best companies to work for as a mum-to-be," Cosmopolitan, 21 January 2019, https://www.cosmopolitan.com/uk/worklife/careers/g21068323/best-uk-companies-maternity-leave/

4 Katie Scott, "GoCompare enhances parental leave policies", Employee Benefits, 26 April 2018, https://www.employeebenefits.co.uk/issues/april-2018/gocompare-parental-leave/

5 Compulsory maternity leave is two weeks long (Employment Rights Act 1996, section 72, and Maternity and Parental Leave Etc Regulations 1999 (SI 1999/3312), regulation 8), but factory workers have four weeks of compulsory maternity leave under the Public Health Act 1936, section 250

time is, if each of the following three conditions is satisfied, modified as mentioned in subsection (5).

(2) The first condition is that, after the time referred to in subsection (1) but before the end of the protected period—

(a) her pay increases, or

(b) it would have increased had she not been on maternity leave.

(3) The second condition is that the maternity-related pay is not —

(a) what her pay would have been had she not been on maternity leave, or

(b) the difference between the amount of statutory maternity pay to which she is entitled and what her pay would have been had she not been on maternity leave.

(4) The third condition is that the terms of her work do not provide for the maternity-related pay to be subject to—

(a) an increase as mentioned in subsection (2)(a), or

(b) an increase that would have occurred as mentioned in subsection (2)(b).

(5) The modification referred to in subsection (1) is a modification to provide for the maternity-related pay to be subject to—

(a) any increase as mentioned in subsection (2)(a), or

(b) any increase that would have occurred as mentioned in subsection (2)(b).

(6) A term of her work that—

(a) provides for pay within subsection (7), but

(b) does not provide for her to be given the pay in circumstances in which she would have been given it had she not been on maternity leave, is modified so as to provide for her to be given it in circumstances in which it would normally be given.

(7) Pay is within this subsection if it is—

(a) pay (including pay by way of bonus) in respect of times before the woman is on maternity leave,

(b) pay by way of bonus in respect of times when she is on compulsory maternity leave, or

(c) pay by way of bonus in respect of times after the end of the protected period.

(8) A term of the woman's work that—

(a) provides for pay after the end of the protected period, but

(b) does not provide for it to be subject to an increase to which it would have been subject had she not been on maternity leave,

is modified so as to provide for it to be subject to the increase.

(9) Maternity-related pay is pay (other than statutory maternity pay) to which a woman is entitled—

(a) as a result of being pregnant, or

(b) in respect of times when she is on maternity leave.

(10) A reference to the protected period is to be construed in accordance with section 18.

Section 75 – Maternity equality rule

Section 75 of the Equality Act 2010 introduces, by automatic operation of law, a maternity equality rule into occupational pension schemes, which gives mothers an important protection of their pension rights, which is their right to receive future pay. The gist of it is that a woman must be treated as a member of the occupational pension scheme even when she is on maternity leave. To remain a member of the occupational pension scheme she does not have to make pension contributions based on her normal level of pay during her maternity leave, although she may be required to make pension contributions based on what she actually earns from the employer during her maternity leave, for those periods of maternity leave when she receives any pay from her employer:

> 75 Maternity equality rule
>
> (1) If an occupational pension scheme does not include a maternity equality rule, it is to be treated as including one.
>
> (2) A maternity equality rule is a provision that has the effect set out in subsections (3) and (4).
>
> (3) If a relevant term does not treat time when the woman is on maternity leave as it treats time when she is not, the term is modified so as to treat time when she is on maternity leave as time when she is not.
>
> (4) If a term confers a relevant discretion capable of being exercised so that time when she is on maternity leave is treated differently from time when she is not, the term is modified so as not to allow the discretion to be exercised in that way.
>
> (5) A term is relevant if it is—
>
> (a) a term relating to membership of the scheme,
>
> (b) a term relating to the accrual of rights under the scheme, or
>
> (c) a term providing for the determination of the amount of a benefit payable under the scheme.
>
> (6) A discretion is relevant if its exercise is capable of affecting—
>
> (a) membership of the scheme,
>
> (b) the accrual of rights under the scheme, or
>
> (c) the determination of the amount of a benefit payable under the scheme.
>
> (7) This section does not require the woman's contributions to the scheme in respect of time when she is on maternity leave to be

determined otherwise than by reference to the amount she is paid in respect of that time.

(8) This section, so far as relating to time when she is on ordinary maternity leave but is not being paid by her employer, applies only in a case where the expected week of childbirth began on or after 6 April 2003.

(9) This section, so far as relating to time when she is on additional maternity leave but is not being paid by her employer—

(a) does not apply to the accrual of rights under the scheme in any case;

(b) applies for other purposes only in a case where the expected week of childbirth began on or after 5 October 2008.

(10) In this section—

(a) a reference to being on maternity leave includes a reference to having been on maternity leave, and

(b) a reference to being paid by the employer includes a reference to receiving statutory maternity pay from the employer.

Section 76 – Exclusion of pregnancy and maternity discrimination provisions

Just as section 70 of the Equality Act 2010 prevents a woman from bringing a sex discrimination claim in regard to unequal pay, so section 76 prevents a mother from bringing a discrimination claim in regard to unequal maternity pay:

76 Exclusion of pregnancy and maternity discrimination provisions

(1) The relevant pregnancy and maternity discrimination provision has no effect in relation to a term of the woman's work that is modified by a maternity equality clause or rule.

(1A) The relevant pregnancy and maternity discrimination provision has no effect in relation to a term of the woman's work—

(a) that relates to pay, but

(b) in relation to which a maternity equality clause or rule has no effect.

(2) The inclusion in the woman's terms of a term that requires modification by virtue of section 73(2) or (3) is not pregnancy and maternity discrimination for the purposes of the relevant pregnancy and maternity discrimination provision.

(3) The relevant pregnancy and maternity discrimination provision is, in relation to a description of work given in the first column of the table, the provision referred to in the second column so far as relating to pregnancy and maternity.

Description of work	**Provision**
Employment	Section 39(2)
Appointment to a personal office	Section 49(6)
Appointment to a public office	Section 50(6)

Section 77 – Discussions about pay

Section 77 of the Equality Act 2010 provided an important precursor to the regime of greater pay transparency which began under the Regulations. It renders void any contractual clauses which seek to gag employees from discussing their pay, stops employers from preventing employees inquiring into one another's pay, and protects employees who make such inquiries against acts of victimisation by the employer:

77 Discussions about pay

(1) A term of a person's work that purports to prevent or restrict the person (P) from disclosing or seeking to disclose information

about the terms of P's work is unenforceable against P in so far as P makes or seeks to make a relevant pay disclosure.

(2) A term of a person's work that purports to prevent or restrict the person (P) from seeking disclosure of information from a colleague about the terms of the colleague's work is unenforceable against P in so far as P seeks a relevant pay disclosure from the colleague; and "colleague" includes a former colleague in relation to the work in question.

(3) A disclosure is a relevant pay disclosure if made for the purpose of enabling the person who makes it, or the person to whom it is made, to find out whether or to what extent there is, in relation to the work in question, a connection between pay and having (or not having) a particular protected characteristic.

(4) The following are to be treated as protected acts for the purposes of the relevant victimisation provision—

(a) seeking a disclosure that would be a relevant pay disclosure;

(b) making or seeking to make a relevant pay disclosure;

(c) receiving information disclosed in a relevant pay disclosure.

(5) The relevant victimisation provision is, in relation to a description of work specified in the first column of the table, section 27 so far as it applies for the purposes of a provision mentioned in the second column.

Description of work	**Provision by virtue of which section 27 has effect**
Employment	Section 39(3) or (4)
Appointment to a personal office	Section 49(5) or (8)
Appointment to a public office	Section 50(5) or (9)

Remedies, Time Limits and Burden of Proof

Having described the current regime for enforcement of the right to equal pay, and before moving on to section 78 of the Equality Act 2010 and pay transparency, it is worth pausing to consider remedies, time limits, and the burden of proof.

Remedies

The principal remedy for a breach of the sex equality clause is damages for breach of contract, which means backpay for up to six years, according to section 132 of the Equality Act 2010:

> 132 Remedies in non-pensions cases
>
> (1) This section applies to proceedings before a court or employment tribunal on a complaint relating to a breach of an equality clause, other than a breach with respect to membership of or rights under an occupational pension scheme.
>
> (2) If the court or tribunal finds that there has been a breach of the equality clause, it may—
>
> (a) make a declaration as to the rights of the parties in relation to the matters to which the proceedings relate;
>
> (b) order an award by way of arrears of pay or damages in relation to the complainant.
>
> (3) The court or tribunal may not order a payment under sub-section (2)(b) in respect of a time before the arrears day.
>
> (4) In relation to proceedings in England and Wales, the arrears day is, in a case mentioned in the first column of the table, the day mentioned in the second column.

Case	Arrears day
A standard case	The day falling 6 years before the day on which the proceedings were instituted.
A concealment case or an incapacity case (or a case which is both).	The day on which the breach first occurred.

(5) In relation to proceedings in Scotland, the arrears day is the first day of—

(a) the period of 5 years ending with the day on which the proceedings were commenced, or

(b) if the case involves a relevant incapacity, or a relevant fraud or error, [the period determined in accordance with section 135(6) and (7)].

Time Limits

There are different limitation periods and rules in Employment Tribunals and the civil courts for this type of breach of contract claim. In the Employment Tribunal, time runs for bringing an equal pay claim for six months from the last day of employment, or from the day on which a stable working relationship ended, or from the day on which the worker discovered or could with reasonable diligence have discovered the qualifying fact in a concealment case, or from the day on which the worker ceased to have an incapacity in an incapacity case, under sections 129 and 130 of the Equality Act 2010. The six-month period is extended to nine months for workers in the armed forces.

Despite the Supreme Court's decision in *Birmingham City Council v Abdulla*[6], that a woman has a free choice whether to bring her equal pay claim in the Employment Tribunal or the civil courts, it remains

6 Birmingham City Council v Abdulla, [2012] UKSC 47; see also Harini Iyengar, "Birmingham City Council v Abdulla (2012)", "Women's Legal Landmarks", Chapter 83, Hart, 2019

extremely rare for equal pay litigation to proceed in the civil courts. This is because of the court fees in the civil courts, the different costs rules, and a widespread respect for the specialist expertise and experience which the Employment Tribunal Judges and Members have built up over many decades, which the civil court Judges tend to lack. Women who do bring equal pay claims in the civil courts benefit from the much longer limitation period for breach of contract claims prescribed in section 5 of the Limitation Act 1980: six years.

The relevant sections provide:

> 129 Time limits
>
> (1) This section applies to—
>
> (a) a complaint relating to a breach of an equality clause or rule;
>
> (b) an application for a declaration referred to in section 127(3) or (4).
>
> (2) Proceedings on the complaint or application may not be brought in an employment tribunal after the end of the qualifying period.
>
> (3) If the complaint or application relates to terms of work other than terms of service in the armed forces, the qualifying period is, in a case mentioned in the first column of the table, the period mentioned in the second column, subject to sections 140A and 140B.

Case	Qualifying period
A standard case	The period of 6 months beginning with the last day of the employment or appointment.
A stable work case (but not if it is also a concealment or incapacity case (or both))	The period of 6 months beginning with the day on which the stable working relationship ended.
A concealment case (but not if it is also an incapacity case)	The period of 6 months beginning with the day on which the worker discovered (or could with reasonable diligence have discovered) the qualifying fact.
An incapacity case (but not if it is also a concealment case)	The period of 6 months beginning with the day on which the worker ceased to have the incapacity.
A case which is a concealment case and an incapacity case.	The period of 6 months beginning with the later of the days on which the period would begin if the case were merely a concealment or incapacity case.

(4) If the complaint or application relates to terms of service in the armed forces, the qualifying period is, in a case mentioned in the first column of the table, the period mentioned in the second column[, subject to section 140B.

Case	Qualifying period
A standard case	The period of 9 months beginning with the last day of the period of service during which the complaint arose.
A concealment case (but not if it is also an incapacity case)	The period of 9 months beginning with the day on which the worker discovered (or could with reasonable diligence have discovered) the qualifying fact.
An incapacity case (but not if it is also a concealment case)	The period of 9 months beginning with the day on which the worker ceased to have the incapacity.
A case which is a concealment case and an incapacity case.	The period of 9 months beginning with the later of the days on which the period would begin if the case were merely a concealment or incapacity case.

and:

130 Section 129: supplementary

(1) This section applies for the purposes of section 129.

(2) A standard case is a case which is not—

(a) a stable work case,

(b) a concealment case,

(c) an incapacity case, or

(d) a concealment case and an incapacity case.

(3) A stable work case is a case where the proceedings relate to a period during which there was a stable working relationship between the worker and the responsible person (including any time after the terms of work had expired).

(4) A concealment case in proceedings relating to an equality clause is a case where—

(a) the responsible person deliberately concealed a qualifying fact from the worker, and

(b) the worker did not discover (or could not with reasonable diligence have discovered) the qualifying fact until after the relevant day.

(5) A concealment case in proceedings relating to an equality rule is a case where—

(a) the employer or the trustees or managers of the occupational pension scheme in question deliberately concealed a qualifying fact from the member, and

(b) the member did not discover (or could not with reasonable diligence have discovered) the qualifying fact until after the relevant day.

(6) A qualifying fact for the purposes of subsection (4) or (5) is a fact—

(a) which is relevant to the complaint, and

(b) without knowledge of which the worker or member could not reasonably have been expected to bring the proceedings.

(7) An incapacity case in proceedings relating to an equality clause with respect to terms of work other than terms of service in the armed forces is a case where the worker had an incapacity during the period of 6 months beginning with the later of—

(a) the relevant day, or

(b) the day on which the worker discovered (or could with reasonable diligence have discovered) the qualifying fact deliberately concealed from the worker by the responsible person.

(8) An incapacity case in proceedings relating to an equality clause with respect to terms of service in the armed forces is a case where the worker had an incapacity during the period of 9 months beginning with the later of—

(a) the last day of the period of service during which the complaint arose, or

(b) the day on which the worker discovered (or could with reasonable diligence have discovered) the qualifying fact deliberately concealed from the worker by the responsible person.

(9) An incapacity case in proceedings relating to an equality rule is a case where the member of the occupational pension scheme in question had an incapacity during the period of 6 months beginning with the later of—

(a) the relevant day, or

(b) the day on which the member discovered (or could with reasonable diligence have discovered) the qualifying fact deliberately concealed from the member by the employer or the trustees or managers of the scheme.

(10) The relevant day for the purposes of this section is—

(a) the last day of the employment or appointment, or

(b) the day on which the stable working relationship between the worker and the responsible person ended.

Burden of Proof

It should also be noted that the burden of proof will be on the woman to prove that she does equal work to her comparator. On the other hand, the employer will have to discharge the burden of proof in relation to any material factor defence which it raises. Under section 136 of the Equality Act 2010, if a claimant provides facts from which the court could decide, in the absence of any other explanation, that the employer contravened the relevant provision of the Equality Act 2010, then the court must hold that the contravention occurred, unless the employer proves that it did not contravene the provision. This is often referred to as a shift in the burden of proof from the employee to the employer.

In practice, however, the outcome of equal pay claims invariably is determined more by the weight of the evidence and the credibility of witnesses, rather than by philosophical arguments about abstract logical proof. It follows that sex discrimination can be inferred in equal pay claims, just it can as in claims of direct or indirect sex discrimination. Therefore, I think that, in a suitable case, an inference of discrimination may be drawn from the manner in which an employer does or avoids collecting, preparing and publishing its gender pay gap reporting figures, or doing an equal pay audit.

Section 136 provides:

> 136 Burden of proof
>
> (1) This section applies to any proceedings relating to a contravention of this Act.
>
> (2) If there are facts from which the court could decide, in the absence of any other explanation, that a person (A) contravened the provision concerned, the court must hold that the contravention occurred.
>
> (3) But subsection (2) does not apply if A shows that A did not contravene the provision.
>
> (4) The reference to a contravention of this Act includes a reference to a breach of an equality clause or rule.
>
> (5) This section does not apply to proceedings for an offence under this Act.
>
> (6) A reference to the court includes a reference to—

(a) an employment tribunal;

(b) the Asylum and Immigration Tribunal;

(c) the Special Immigration Appeals Commission;

(d) the First-tier Tribunal;

(e) the Special Educational Needs Tribunal for Wales Education Tribunal for Wales;

(f) the First-tier Tribunal for Scotland Health and Education Chamber.

An overview of the cumbersome and eccentric equal pay provisions, which apply exclusively to unequal pay because of sex, provides a glimpse into the procedural and substantive legal obstacles which women workers face in enforcing their right to equal pay for equal work. These barriers are often unsurmountable for women workers who do not have financial access to expert legal representation to guide them through this complex area of law. These difficulties have heavily restricted the role which litigation could have played in reducing unequal pay between men and women in the British labour market since the Equal Pay Act 1970 came into force in 1975. In turn, the persistence and prevalence of unlawful unequal pay between men and women in the labour market have influenced the very slow rate at which the gender pay gap is closing in Britain. Equal pay litigation and sex discrimination litigation have been demonstrated not to be an effective method for closing the gender pay gap.

CHAPTER SIX
THE LEGAL AND POLITICAL BACKGROUND TO THE EQUALITY ACT 2010 (GENDER PAY GAP INFORMATION) REGULATIONS 2017

Summary: In this chapter, I move on to discuss section 78 of the Equality Act 2010 on pay transparency and the rules on mandatory gender pay gap reporting contained in the Equality Act 2010 (Gender Pay Gap Information Reporting) Regulations 2017.

The Equality Act 2010 was a huge piece of consolidating and reforming equalities legislation passed by Parliament. Section 78 contained a brand new landmark provision requiring employers to publish gender pay gap information:

> 78 Gender pay gap information
>
> (1) Regulations may require employers to publish information relating to the pay of employees for the purpose of showing whether, by reference to factors of such description as is prescribed, there are differences in the pay of male and female employees.
>
> (2) This section does not apply to—
>
> (a) an employer who has fewer than 250 employees;
>
> (b) a person specified in Schedule 19;
>
> (c) a government department or part of the armed forces not specified in that Schedule.
>
> (3) The regulations may prescribe—
>
> (a) descriptions of employer;

(b) descriptions of employee;

(c) how to calculate the number of employees that an employer has;

(d) descriptions of information;

(e) the time at which information is to be published;

(f) the form and manner in which it is to be published.

(4) Regulations under subsection (3)(e) may not require an employer, after the first publication of information, to publish information more frequently than at intervals of 12 months.

(5) The regulations may make provision for a failure to comply with the regulations—

(a) to be an offence punishable on summary conviction by a fine not exceeding level 5 on the standard scale;

(b) to be enforced, otherwise than as an offence, by such means as are prescribed.

(6) The reference to a failure to comply with the regulations includes a reference to a failure by a person acting on behalf of an employer.

Nevertheless, for several years, section 78 remained on the statute book without being brought into force by Parliament.

In September 2011, the Government launched a voluntary gender pay gap reporting scheme, called "Think, Act, Report"[1]. By August 2014, just four employers had published their gender pay gap data the scheme[2]. On 5 November 2014, the GEO published a report, "The

1 Theresa May, "Home Secretary's speech on new equality reporting scheme for businesses", 14 September 2011, https://www.gov.uk/government/speeches/home-secretarys-speech-on-new-equality-reporting-scheme-for-businesses

2 Rajeev Syal, "Just four companies reveal gender pay gap under coalition scheme", The Guardian, 12 August 2014, https://www.theguardian.com/money/2014/aug/12/gender-pay-gap-coalition-scheme

Gender Pay Gap Matters"[3], in partnership with "everywoman" organisation, and announced that 260 companies had signed up to the voluntary "Think, Act, Report" initiative which "encourage[d] companies to think (sic) about gender equality in the workplace."

There was little political will in Government to make publication of gender pay gap information mandatory rather than merely voluntary. The backbench female Opposition Member of Parliament, Sarah Champion, however, argued that the "Think, Act, Report" initiative left equal pay as a worthless promise[4]. On 16 December 2014, she won, by a large majority, a vote on her Ten Minute Rule Bill to bring section 78 of the Equality Act 2010 finally into force, which created media interest and a pressure on Government.

Section 147 of the Small Business, Enterprise and Employment Act 2015, enacted on 26 March 2015, then required pay transparency regulations to be made by 25 March 2016. It provided:

> 147 Equal pay: transparency
>
> a) The Secretary of State must, as soon as possible, and no later than 12 months after the passing of this Act, make regulations under section 178 of the Equality Act 2010 (gender pay gap information) for the purpose of requiring the publication of information showing whether there are differences in the pay of males and females.
>
> b) The Secretary of State must consult such persons as the Secretary of State thinks appropriate on the details of such regulations prior to publication.

---

3 Government Equalities Office, "Press Release", 5 November 2014, https://www.gov.uk/government/news/government-announces-2-million-fund-to-help-close-gender-pay-gap including jointly with "everywoman" "The Gender Pay Gap Matters", https://www.everywoman.com/sites/default/files/file/GEO-online%20-march%202015.pdf

4 BBC, "MPs back gender disclosure obligation for big firms", 16 December 2014, https://www.bbc.co.uk/news/uk-politics-30495223

The Government launched a seven-week public consultation from 14 July 2015 on "Closing the gender pay gap". On 12 February 2016, the Government published a second report for consultation, accompanied this time by draft regulations. The only question was whether any modifications should be made to the ten draft regulations, and the short consultation period closed on 11 March 2016. The House of Commons Women and Equalities Committee then published a further Report on 22 March 2016[5]. Despite the 25 March 2016 deadline, the measures were delayed by Parliament.

The Equality Act 2010 (Gender Pay Gap Information) Regulations 2017 were eventually made on 6 February 2017 and commenced on 6 April 2017. The first round of information had to be published by 5 April 2018. In my view, a decade's progress has been lost by the delay caused by Parliament's stalling implementation of section 78 of the Equality Act 2010, because it is only when one examines a few years' worth of gender pay gap information across the labour market, within specific industry sectors, and within individual organisations, that one can find meaningful trends, understand them, and then take effective steps to address any unfairnesses or inequalities which the trends have revealed.

5 Women and Equalities Committee, "Gender Pay Gap", 22 March 2016 https://www.parliament.uk/business/committees/committees-a-z/commons-select/women-and-equalities-committee/inquiries/parliament-2015/gender-pay-gap-15-16/

CHAPTER SEVEN
THE EQUALITY ACT 2010 (GENDER PAY GAP INFORMATION) REGULATIONS 2017

Summary: In this chapter, I set out one by one the regulations provided in the Equality Act 2010 (Gender Pay Gap Information) Regulations 2017 and explain what they require, including some commentary and some references to available guidance. At the time of writing, no cases concerning the meaning or interpretation of the Regulations have come before the courts yet.

The role of the Advisory, Conciliation and Arbitration Service, known as ACAS, is to provide free and impartial information and advice to employers and employees on all aspects of workplace relations and employment law, and to support good relationships between employers and employees. Where required, ACAS also offers a conciliation service to resolve workplace disputes, including the early conciliation process required before presentation of equal pay claims in the Employment Tribunal. ACAS is governed by a Council consisting of a Chair and eleven members from employer, trade union and independent backgrounds, in paid public appointments made by the Secretary of State for Business, Energy and Industrial Strategy. ACAS is now offering employers Gender Pay Gap Reporting Training services.

The GEO has responsibilities which include policy relating to women, taking the lead on the Equality Act 2010 and gender issues. On 16 November 2018 the UK Government announced that the GEO would be transferring to the Cabinet Office from 1 April 2019, in accordance with recommendations from the Women and Equalities Select Committee[1].

---

1 Penny Mordaunt, "Oral Statement to Parliament", "Government Equalities Office to join Cabinet Office", 16 November 2018,

At the time of writing, the GEO's strategic priorities[2] included:

- helping women to fulfil their potential in the workplace and helping businesses get the full economic benefit of women's skills
- eliminating the Gender Pay Gap (GPG) by introducing regulations requiring larger employers to publish their gender pay data, and working with other government departments to address the causes of the GPG
- improving female career progression, increasing the number of women on government boards, and in the FTSE 350
- supporting cross-government strategies, such as; increasing female participation in the labour market, and preventing violence against women and girls (VAWG)

In February 2019, ACAS and the GEO jointly published non-statutory guidance called "Managing gender pay gap reporting"[3], which is not intended to be used as a substitute for legal advice ("the ACAS/GEO Guidance"). In addition to setting out the legal obligations imposed by the Regulations, the guidance includes advice from ACAS on good employment practice.

---

https://www.gov.uk/government/speeches/government-equalities-office-to-join-cabinet-office

2 Government Equalities Office, "About", https://www.gov.uk/government/organisations/government-equalities-office/about

3 ACAS and Government Equalities Office, "Managing Gender Pay Gap Reporting", 7 February 2019, http://www.acas.org.uk/media/pdf/9/p/Managing_gender_pay_reporting_07.02.19.pdf

Regulation 1 – Citation, commencement and interpretation

1 Citation, commencement and interpretation

(1) These Regulations may be cited as the Equality Act 2010 (Gender Pay Gap Information) Regulations 2017 and come into force on 6th April 2017.

(2) In these Regulations—

"bonus pay" has the meaning given in regulation 4;

"full-pay relevant employee" means a relevant employee who is not, during the relevant pay period, being paid at a reduced rate or nil as a result of the employee being on leave;

"hourly rate of pay" has the meaning given in regulation 6;

"ITEPA 2003" means the Income Tax (Earnings and Pensions) Act 2003;

"leave" includes—

(a) annual leave;

(b) maternity, paternity, adoption, parental or shared parental leave;

(c) sick leave; and

(d) special leave;

"ordinary pay" has the meaning given in regulation 3;

"pay period" has the meaning given in regulation 5(1);

"piecework" means work in respect of which an employee is entitled to be paid by reference to a number of pieces made or processed, or a number of tasks performed, instead of by reference to a period of time worked;

"relevant employee" means (subject to paragraph (4)) a person who is employed by the relevant employer on the snapshot date;

"relevant employer" means (subject to paragraph (6)) an employer who has 250 or more employees on the snapshot date;

"relevant pay period" has the meaning given in regulation 5(2);

"snapshot date" means the 5th April in the year to which the information required by regulation 2 relates.

(3) For the purposes of these Regulations, the amount of an employee's ordinary pay or bonus pay is to be calculated before deductions made at source (for example deductions in relation to income tax).

(4) In paragraph (2), a "relevant employee" does not include a partner in a firm.

(5) For the purposes of paragraph (4)—

(a) "firm" has the same meaning as in the Income Tax (Trading and Other Income) Act 2005, and

(b) "partner" includes a member of a limited liability partnership to which section 863(1) of the Income Tax (Trading and Other Income) Act 2005 applies.

(6) In paragraph (2), a "relevant employer" does not include—

(a) a person specified in Schedule 19 to the Equality Act 2010; or

(b) a government department or part of the armed forces not specified in that Schedule

Regulation 1 contains a set of key definitions under the Regulations and provided for the Regulations to come into force on 6 April 2017.

Under regulation 1(2), a "relevant employee" is someone employed by the "relevant employer" during the relevant "pay period". A "relevant employer" is one with 250 or more employees on the "snapshot date" of 5 April in the relevant gender pay gap reporting year.

Under section 83(2)(a) of the Equality Act 2010, the meaning of the legal term "employee" is a wider an "extended" meaning of "employee" which goes beyond the definition under the Employment Rights Act 1996:

83 Interpretation and exceptions

...

(3) "Employment" means –

(a) employment under a contract of employment, a contract of apprenticeship or a contract personally to do work;

...

Employment status is a complex and changing area within employment law. Workers who benefit from the status of "employee" enjoy enhanced statutory entitlements above other workers in many important and valuable respects, including protections against unfair dismissal and redundancy, and certain rights associated with pregnancy, maternity and parenthood. It should be remembered that the Regulations concern "employees" only, and that despite the extended definition of "employee" which applies here, it is not necessarily the case that all "workers" within the meaning of European Union law are necessarily "employees" within the meaning of the Equality Act 2010.

As the labour market has changed in recent years to leave many more workers in more precarious forms of work, such as agency work, zero hours contracts, and questionable self-employed status, it is, unsurprisingly, typically the most vulnerable workers who benefit the least from any enhancements to the protections enjoyed by "employees", and who are most likely to lack the resources to bring a legal case to prove that they are "employees". To the extent that the Regulations enhance the right to equal pay for equal work which "employees" enjoy, it should not be forgotten that many workers in the British labour market, because they do not meet the legal definition of "employee", are excluded from the right to equal pay and from the gender pay gap reporting regime. Thus, some organisations, for example, carework agencies, nursing locum services, or taxi or plumbing firms which may have many "self-employed" staff whom they do not count as "employees" within the meaning of the law, will not find the Regulations to be the correct tool for understanding the reality of any pay inequalities within their own organisations.

Significant definitions within Regulation 1 include "full-pay relevant employee", which means a relevant employee who is not, during the relevant pay period, being paid at a reduced rate or nil as a result of the employee being on leave. In the scheme of the Regulations, "leave" includes annual leave, maternity, paternity, adoption, parental or shared parental leave, sick leave and special leave.

Thus, pay differences which arise from reduced rates of pay during leave which the employee takes because of parenthood are not picked up by the Regulations. Yet, as was discussed in Chapter One, across the labour market, unpaid childcare responsibilities which women fulfil and the lower pay received during maternity leave play a significant role in the gender pay gap and the reduced retention in employment of mothers compared to fathers.

Similarly, for example, disabled employees often have greater periods of sickness absence than non-disabled employees, and may benefit from reasonable adjustments under the Equality Act 2010 which acknowledge that reality and protect them against detrimental treatment because of sickness absences related to their disabilities. Nevertheless, any greater pay disadvantage faced by disabled women employees where their rate of sick pay is less than full pay will not be shown in the compulsory gender pay gap reporting data.

Therefore, employers who genuinely wish to understand, for example, pay patterns of working mothers and disabled women – or other kinds of intersectional disadvantage which women employees in their organisation may be facing – would need to go beyond the Regulations in order to find helpful pay data which could inform positive action to help working mothers and disabled women to thrive in the workforce.

Regulation 1(4) expressly excludes a partner in a firm from the definition of "relevant employee". Under regulation 1(5), "firm" has the same meaning as in the Income Tax (Trading and Other Income) Act 2005 and "partner" includes a member of a limited liability partnership to which section 863(1) of the Income Tax (Trading and Other Income) Act 2005 applies. Thus, there is no legal obligation to include partners of firms in the gender pay gap reporting data, even though some of the widest gender pay gaps in the British labour market exist at the most senior levels in highly-skilled occupations.

In March 2018, Britain's "Big Four" audit firms, PwC, Deloitte, KPMG and EY, were heavily criticised in the media[4] for submitting gender pay gap information which excluded their equity partners, who were overwhelmingly male, and thus gave an artificial impression of the gender pay gap in their organisations. In response, they voluntarily revealed new figures which included partners' remuneration. Although peer pressure and press interest can in this way achieve transparency in the case of the largest employers on a voluntary basis, it is vital to remember that the Regulations do not require gender pay gap information to be submitted on partners, and many smaller and less conspicuous businesses will continue to take advantage of the exclusion of partners from the Regulations, either by not examining the pay of partners at all, or by keeping those figures confidential and for internal purposes only.

The House of Commons Business, Energy and Industrial Strategy Committee was disappointed that the six "Magic Circle" law firms did not follow the example of voluntary publication of partner gender pay gap information set by the Big Four. The Committee wrote directly asking for their gender pay gap and partner remuneration data, which

4 Madison Marriage, "Big four accountants grapple with gender pay gaps", Financial Times, 30 March 2018, https://www.ft.com/content/4625c9b2-2e96-11e8-9b4b-bc4b9f08f381

revealed "in every case significantly higher" gender pay gaps when partners were included[5].

It is notable that in its guidance to the solicitors' profession, "Gender pay gap reporting: Setting the standard for the profession"[6], on 6 November 2018, the Law Society recommended that firms should adopt a best practice approach, including: firms with fewer than 250 employees voluntarily reporting on their gender pay gap data where it is practicable to do so; partner remuneration data being included; gender pay gap data also being reported by comparing full-time equivalent total compensation over a year not just on the snapshot date; including all staff working in subsidiary entities in England, Scotland or Wales; including a robust narrative report; including a detailed action plan; and collecting data on disability, ethnicity and sexuality pay gaps.

The ACAS/GEO Guidance advises that partners, where they would usually also be considered employees, should be used to establish the employee headcount, which if 250 or above would make gender pay gap reporting mandatory, but that partners' earnings should not be used in the gender pay gap information. It says:

> Organisations that want to voluntarily include partners in their calculations can publish them separately in their narrative or on their website.
>
> ...
>
> Provided that the legally required calculations are clearly provided, employers can enhance their reports as they wish on a voluntary basis where they consider this informative and appropriate. In most cases, this will be through supplying additional information in the voluntary narrative that accompanies a published report.

---

5 House of Commons, Business Energy and Industrial Strategy Committee, "Thirteenth Report of Session 2017-2019", 23 July 2018, https://publications.parliament.uk/pa/cm201719/cmselect/cmbeis/928/928.pdf

6 https://www.lawsociety.org.uk/support-services/advice/articles/gender-pay-gap-reporting-setting-the-standard/

Regulation 1(3) makes clear that the employee's ordinary or bonus pay is to be calculated before deductions are made at source for items such as income tax.

Excluded from the definition of "relevant employer" by regulation 1(6)(a) are persons specified in Schedule 19 to the Equality Act 2010, which is a long list of public authorities, on whom the public sector equality duty is imposed by section 149 of the Equality Act 2010. Further, regulation 1(6)(b) makes clear that any government department or part of the armed forces which is not listed in Schedule 19 is also not a relevant employer. Public bodies with over 250 employees are covered by the Equality Act 2010 (Specific Duties and Public Authorities) Regulations 2017 (SI 2017/353), as part of their public sector equality duty under section 149 of the Equality Act 2010. The main practical difference is that the "snapshot" reporting date is 30 March each year, not 5 April, and the Equality Act 2010 (Specific Duties and Public Authorities) Regulations 2017 are not considered separately in this book.

Regulation 2 – Duty to publish annual information relating to pay

2 Duty to publish annual information relating to pay

(1) A relevant employer must publish, for 2017 and each subsequent year, the following information—

(a) the difference between the mean hourly rate of pay of male full-pay relevant employees and that of female full-pay relevant employees (see regulation 8);

(b) the difference between the median hourly rate of pay of male full-pay relevant employees and that of female full-pay relevant employees (see regulation 9);

(c) the difference between the mean bonus pay paid to male relevant employees and that paid to female relevant employees (see regulation 10);

(d) the difference between the median bonus pay paid to male relevant employees and that paid to female relevant employees (see regulation 11);

(e) the proportions of male and female relevant employees who were paid bonus pay (see regulation 12); and

(f) the proportions of male and female full-pay relevant employees in the lower, lower middle, upper middle and upper quartile pay bands (see regulation 13).

(2) The relevant employer must publish the information required by paragraph (1) within the period of 12 months beginning with the snapshot date.

(3) In compiling the information required by paragraph (1), the relevant employer is not required to include data relating to a relevant employee if—

(a) the employee is employed under a contract personally to do work, and

(b) the employer does not have, and it is not reasonably practicable for the employer to obtain, the data.

Regulation 2 sets out the publication duties upon employers. From the original snapshot date of 5 April 2017 onwards, the employer is required to publish information annually, showing nine statistics for their workforce. The publication must be within 12 months of 5 April each year. Generally, most companies are leaving it until just before the 5 April deadline to submit their reports, although, once the gender pay gap reporting systems are in place internally, there should be no particular reason to delay publication of the figures. Leaving insufficient time to assess the figures and prepare a supporting narrative exposes an employer to a greater risk of public criticism than a well-scheduled approach.

An exception is made in regulation 2(3)(a), which narrows the scope of the duty to publish, by excluding self-employed employees who are "employed under a contract personally to do work" for whom the employer does not have the data and does not find it reasonably practicable to obtain the data.

The nine statistics which must be published are:

1. The difference between the mean hourly rate of pay of male full-pay relevant employees and female full-pay relevant employees

2. The difference between the median hourly rate of pay of male full-pay relevant employees and female full-pay relevant employees

3. The difference between the mean bonus pay of male relevant employees and female relevant employees

4. The difference between the median bonus pay of male relevant employees and female relevant employees

5. The proportions of male relevant employees who were paid bonus pay and female relevant employees who were paid bonus pay

6. The proportion of male and female full-pay relevant employees in the lower quartile band

7. The proportion of male and female full-pay relevant employees in the lower middle quartile band

8. The proportion of male and female full-pay relevant employees in the upper middle quartile band

9. The proportion of male and female full-pay relevant employees in the upper quartile band

Many of the immediately-apparent errors by employers in the data which is displayed on the Government's gender pay gap reporting website, which commentators describe as "statistically highly-improbable" appear to have arisen from basic mathematical mistakes and misunderstandings. The annual cost of low adult numeracy to Britain by employers is £3.2 billion; by individuals including employees, it is £8.8 billion; and by Government it is £8.2 billion[7]. Therefore, since this book is aimed at a wide audience, I make no apology for including these reminders about how to calculate the difference between the mean and the median average hourly rates of pay for male and female employees and what the gender pay gap reporting figures represent.

At the outset, imagine that the employer calls a big meeting of everyone who works in the organisation on 5 April. It is then announced that only "employees" can stay for the rest of the session; those who are employed under a contract personally to do work can join in only if the employer already has their pay data or finds it reasonably practicable to obtain the data so that they can join in. Next, anyone who is classed as officially on leave during the relevant pay period, will be asked to exit the meeting, if they are being paid at a reduced hourly rate because of their leave. Even if she is present at work on a "keeping in touch" day, under regulation 12A of the Maternity and Parental Leave etc Regulations 1999[8] anyone who is on maternity, paternity, adoption or shared parental pay will not be allowed to join in, unless she is on full pay during the relevant pay period.

The ACAS/GEO Guidance gives these examples:

> For example... Full-pay relevant employee Jalissa, Jenny, Jakob, Jackie, Jill and Javed all do the same role on the same terms and conditions, work five days a week, get paid weekly, and would usually earn £400 basic pay in the relevant pay period.
>
> - Jalissa worked all week and earned £400. This means she is a full-pay relevant employee.

7 Pro Bono Economics, "Cost of Outcomes Associated with Low Levels of Adult Numeracy in the UK", 2014, http://www.nationalnumeracy.org.uk/resources/135/index.html

8 SI 1999/3312

- Jenny worked four days but took a fifth day as fully paid special leave to deal with a childcare-related emergency and earned £400. This means she is a full-pay relevant employee.
- Jakob worked four days but took a fifth day as unpaid special leave to attend a funeral and earned £320. This counts as leave and Jakob earned less than usual so he is not a full-pay relevant employee.
- Jackie was off all week but took fully paid annual leave, so she still earned £400. This counts as leave and she still earned her usual pay, so she is a full-pay relevant employee.
- Jill was on maternity leave and received statutory maternity pay, which wasl ess than £400. This counts as leave and because Jill earned less than usual, she is not a full-pay relevant employee.
- Javed worked three days and was involved in official strike action for two daysand earned £240. Although Javed earned less than usual, this does not count as leave so he would still be a full-pay relevant employee.
- Another colleague, Jade, carries out the same role in a part-time arrangement where she works the equivalent of three days per week, earning £240. She worked all her hours in the relevant pay period. This means she is a full-pay relevant employee.

Note: Even though they are not full-pay relevant employees, Jakob and Jill would still be 'relevant employees', so while they would not be included in the gender pay gap calculations involving an hourly rate of pay, they would still be included in the bonus gender pay gap calculations.

The mean hourly rate of pay for male full-pay relevant employees is worked out by adding up all the hourly rates of pay of the male full-pay relevant employees and dividing by the number of full-pay relevant male employees. A simple way to visualise this is to imagine all the relevant full-pay male employees in the organisation bringing an hour's pay with them in cash to a big meeting, placing all the money on the boardroom table, and then sharing the total cash out equally between all the men in the room. Likewise, the mean hourly rate of pay of the female full-pay relevant employees is calculated by adding up all the hourly rates of pay of the full-pay relevant female employees and dividing by the number of female full-pay relevant employees. To obtain the difference, the mean average hourly rate of pay of the female full-pay relevant employees must be subtracted from the mean average hourly rate of pay of the male full-pay relevant employees and the result is expressed as a percentage of the mean average hourly rate of pay of the male full-pay relevant employees. This can be visualised by imagining a male colleague, who had left his meeting with his share of the cash earlier that day, later meeting up with a female colleague who has just left her meeting with her share of the cash, and her asking him to show her how much more money he has in his pocket, compared to how much money she has. The difference between the money in their pockets must be expressed as a percentage of the pay in his pocket.

Thus, in the majority of cases in the British labour market, where the men's average hourly rate of pay is higher than the women's, the subtraction will give a positive number, which shows that there is a gender pay gap. If, however, the men's average hourly rate of pay in a particular organisation is lower than the women's average hourly rate of pay (which is most often observed in low-paid, part-time female-dominated sectors such as care work or cleaning) then the subtraction will produce a minus number, demonstrating what is called a negative gender pay gap. A positive gender pay gap should lead employers and employees to question why women in their organisation are earning less than men in their organisation; and a negative gender pay gap should lead employers and employees to question why men in their organisation are earning less than women in their organisation.

The median average hourly rate of pay for male full-pay relevant employees is obtained by putting all of the average hourly rates figures of the male full-pay relevant employees into ascending or descending order, and picking out the middle value in the series. A simple way to visualise the median average hourly rate of pay of male full-pay relevant employees is to imagine all the men leaving their meeting in the boardroom and then going out into the carpark, each holding a placard on which his hourly rate of pay is written, then organising themselves into a long line, in order of the number value written on their placards, and next counting inwards from both ends of the long line, to find the man who is standing right in the middle of the long line: the hourly rate of pay written on his placard will be the median average hourly rate of pay for the male full-pay relevant employees. If two men are standing exactly in the middle of the long line, then the median average hourly rate of pay for male full-pay relevant employees will be the mean average of the two hourly rates of pay of those two men.

Then, imagine all the female full-pay relevant employees performing the same exercise. The difference required to be reported is obtained by taking away the number written on the chosen woman's placard from the number written on the chosen man's placard, and expressing it as a percentage of the figure written on his placard.

The gender pay gap reporting regime devised by the Regulations is crude and rough. The data gives a broad overview of the major differences between male and female employees' pay. The figures obtained will not tell employers or employees sophisticated information about exactly why certain groups of women employees may be earning less in their workforce: it will not reveal any subtleties affecting women's training, development or career progression within the organisation and it will not demonstrate whether pay inequality arises from any other factors of intersectional disadvantage, for example, pregnancy or maternity, childcare or domestic responsibilities, race, disability, lone parent status, domestic violence, or disability.

Conversely, the fact that an organisation's gender pay gap appears to be in line with the pay gap reported by other employers in the same industry sector cannot be taken as a reassurance that there is no unlawful pay inequality or unlawful sex discrimination blighting women's careers within the employer's workforce.

A similar calculation method is used in order to work out the difference between the mean average bonus pay of the male relevant employees who were paid bonus pay during the previous year and mean average bonus pay of the female relevant employees who were paid bonus pay during the previous year, and express it as a percentage of the mean average bonus pay of the male relevant employees who were paid bonus pay during the previous year. Likewise, a similar calculation method is used in order to work out the percentage difference between the median average bonus pay received by each of the two sexes of the relevant employees who received bonus pay during the relevant period. The bonus gender pay gap calculations concern all relevant employees during the previous year who received bonus pay, and do not involve all "relevant employees" nor all "full-pay relevant employees", unless they all received bonus pay.

The references to the proportions of men and women who were paid bonus pay are references to the respective fractions of men and women receiving bonus pay out of the total number of relevant employees of each sex. A simple way to visualise this is to imagine that all the male relevant employees are put into a room, the number of men amongst them who received bonus pay during the last year is counted and it is expressed as a percentage of all the men in the room; meanwhile, all the female relevant employees are put into a room, the number of women amongst them who received bonus pay during the last year is counted and it is expressed as a percentage of all the women in the room.

The same approach applies to calculating the proportions of men and women in each of the quartile bands. The quartile bands provide a simplistic method for beginning to explore why a workforce may have a gender pay gap and how it relates to occupational segregation or vertical stratification within the organisation. By dividing the workforce into quartile bands, different gender pay gaps are typically revealed at different levels in the pay hierarchy.

A way to visualise this is to imagine that every full-pay relevant employee in the organisation brings a placard to the carpark on which is written their hourly rate of pay. They all line up in order of the number value on their placard. Then, the long line is divided up into four equal smaller lines. Within each of the smaller lines, the proportion of male and female relevant employees is calculated.

This exercise of dividing the workforce into quartile bands often reveals patterns. For example, in a consumer retail business, it may show that in the lower quartile nearly all the workers are female because the shop floor workers are nearly all women whereas in the lower middle quartile, the warehouse staff may be nearly all men, in the upper middle quartile the team leaders and middle managers may be nearly all men, and in the upper quartile, the head office managers are all male. Or, say, in a public authority, there may be a good balance of men and women in the lower quartile, because even though there is occupational segregation between road sweepers and school lunchtime meals assistants, their rate of pay is similar, however, there may be more women in the lower middle quartile band, because women are over-represented amongst administrative staff and social care staff, whereas in the upper quartile, there may be a preponderance of men in the highest-paid and most senior leadership roles. Taking an overview of gender balance across the whole workforce at once would not reveal these patterns. In response to seeing these patterns emerge, an employer may, for instance, reflect upon why fewer women were progressing through to the highest levels of pay and leadership, even though the employer was a good recruiter and retainer of women workers in the lower-paid and less senior roles.

Regulation 3 – Meaning of "ordinary pay"

3 Meaning of "ordinary pay"

(1) In these Regulations, "ordinary pay" means (subject to paragraph (2))—

(a) basic pay;

(b) allowances;

(c) pay for piecework;

(d) pay for leave;

(e) shift premium pay.

(2) "Ordinary pay" does not include—

(a) remuneration referable to overtime,

(b) remuneration referable to redundancy or termination of employment,

(c) remuneration in lieu of leave, or

(d) remuneration provided otherwise than in money.

(3) In paragraph (1)—

(a) "allowances" includes any sum paid with respect to—

(i) any duty of the employee, such as a duty in connection with the role of fire or bomb warden, that is ancillary to the main duties of the employee's employment;

(ii) the location of the employment in a particular area;

(iii) the purchase, lease or maintenance of a vehicle;

(iv) the recruitment and retention of an employee; and

(v) the purchase, lease or maintenance of an item;

but excludes any payment to reimburse expenditure wholly and necessarily incurred by the employee in the course of his or her employment.

(b) "shift premium pay" means the difference between basic pay and any higher rate paid by the employer for work during different times of the day or night.

Regulation 3 contains the vitally important definition of "ordinary pay". "Ordinary pay" means basic pay, allowances, pay for piecework, pay for leave and shift premium pay. "Allowances" are defined as including any sum paid with respect to any duty of the employee which is ancillary to the employee's main duties (such as any duty in connection with the role of a fire warden or bomb warden), the location of the employment in a particular area, the purchase, lease or maintenance of a vehicle, the recruitment and retention of an employee and the purchase, lease or maintenance of an item. Allowances exclude any payment to reimburse expenditure wholly or necessarily incurred by the employee in the course of his or her employment. In everyday language, ordinary pay includes allowances for special duties like being a fire-warden, location allowance, car allowance, golden hellos, retention bonuses, and the provision of certain items as "perks" (perquisites), but it excludes payments from the employer to the employee for items such as expenses, season ticket loans, redundancy payments, arrears of wages and money which the employee may receive through tax credits. Although, in practice, nearly all employees receive their pay from their employer net of income tax, it is the gross pay figures which are used for the Regulations.

The effects of the income tax regime and in-work-benefits welfare system, and their interaction with each other, have important practical impacts upon the way in which men and women select and remain in different jobs. What people earn at work is very different from the disposable income which they have in their pockets available to spend. I consider that tax and benefits have important knock-on effects upon the spending money in the pockets of male full-pay relevant employees and female full-pay relevant employees, and on employers' ability to recruit and retain women in certain jobs, however, it must be noted that those effects will not be picked up by the gender pay gap reporting regime, because it uses gross pay figures, not take home pay figures or disposable income figures.

The ACAS/GEO Guidance advises that the value of any benefits provided under a "salary sacrifice" scheme should be excluded from "ordinary pay". Some employers have felt this to be unfair, particularly where they regarded the salary sacrifice scheme as helpful for retaining mothers in the workforce, for example, where the scheme offered subsidised workplace childcare. On the other hand, such schemes do ultimately reduce the take-home pay of the employee, and the employer always has the option to accompany the gender pay gap reporting figures with a narrative which explains some of the reasons for the gender pay gap in its organisation and any equal pay action plan which it operates.

"Ordinary pay" includes pay for piecework, pay for leave and shift premium pay, which is the difference between basic pay and the rate paid by the employer for work at different times of the day or night. Excluded from the definition of "ordinary pay" is remuneration referable to overtime, redundancy or termination, pay in lieu of leave, and remuneration otherwise than in money. The exclusion of overtime pay is particularly notable, because in the British labour market, men generally have a greater opportunity than women to perform overtime, because women are more likely to perform unpaid childcare and domestic labour which makes them unavailable for paid overtime work. Since men are more likely to work anti-social hours, being less likely to take on childcare and domestic responsibilities, shift premium pay is an important aspect of the gender pay gap in the British labour market. The increased pay which male employees gain from overtime work is not measured by the Regulations and employers which would like to examine and understand the effect of long working hours within their workforce upon the gender pay gap may have to obtain data which goes beyond the scope of the Regulations.

Regulation 4 – Meaning of "bonus pay"

4 Meaning of "bonus pay"

(1) In these Regulations, "bonus pay" means (subject to paragraph (2)) any remuneration that—

(a) is in the form of money, vouchers, securities, securities options, or interests in securities,

(b) relates to profit sharing, productivity, performance, incentive or commission.

(2) "Bonus pay" does not include—

(a) ordinary pay,

(b) remuneration referable to overtime, or

(c) remuneration referable to redundancy or termination of employment.

(3) For the purpose of paragraph (1), remuneration in the form of securities, securities options and interests in securities is to be treated as paid to the employee at the time, and in the amounts in respect of which, the securities, securities options and interests in securities give rise to (or would give rise to, if the employee were an employee for the purposes of Part 2 of ITEPA 2003 (employment income))—

(a) any taxable earnings within the meaning of section 10(2) of ITEPA 2003; or

(b) any taxable specific income within the meaning of section 10(3) of ITEPA 2003.

(4) In this regulation, "securities", "securities options" and "interests in securities" have thein same meaning as in section 420 of ITEPA 2003.

Regulation 4 defines "bonus pay". It is remuneration which is not ordinary pay, and which is in the form of money, vouchers, securities, securities options or interests in securities, and which relates to profit sharing, productivity, performance, incentive or commission. Unusually, there is neither "and" nor "or" between regulation 4(1)(a) and 4(1)(b). For the simple reason that it is hard to think of any other form which the remuneration could take, beyond the money, vouchers, securities, securities options or interests in securities mentioned in regulation 4(1)(a), I have concluded that an "and" has most likely been omitted in error; but I await with interest a test case involving bonus pay in cryptocurrency! Bonus pay excludes ordinary pay, overtime pay, redundancy pay or other pay referable to termination.

Interesting questions arise for employers about particular bonus schemes in which the right to exercise a securities option arises by an event referable to termination or the termination itself, however, the Regulations provide no enforcement or audit mechanism by which employees could easily discover whether their employer had misinterpreted Regulation 4 and excluded an element of bonus pay in error. Bonus pay in the form of share schemes (securities, securities options or interests in securities) is treated as paid to the employee or former employee on the date at which it gives rise to taxable earnings or taxable specific income within the meaning of the relevant taxation legislation.

Regulation 5 – Meaning of the "pay period" and the "relevant pay period"

> 5 Meaning of the "pay period" and the "relevant pay period"
>
> (1) In these Regulations, the "pay period", in relation to a relevant employee, means—
>
> (a) the period in respect of which the relevant employer pays the employee basic pay, whether weekly, fortnightly, monthly or any other period, or
>
> (b) if the relevant employer does not pay the employee basic pay, the period in respect of which the employer most frequently pays the employee one of the elements of ordinary pay mentioned in regulation 3(1)(b) to (e).

(2) In these Regulations, the "relevant pay period" means the pay period within which the snapshot date falls.

Regulation 5 defines the relevant "pay period" for which the relevant employee's hourly pay will be calculated. In most cases, it is simply the period in respect of which the employer pays the employee basic pay, namely, weekly, fortnightly, monthly, or any other period. If the employer does not pay the employee basic pay, then the "pay period" is the period in respect of which the employer most frequently pays the employee allowances, pay for piecework, pay for leave or shift premium pay. Where reference is made in the Regulations to the "relevant pay period", it means the pay period within which the snapshot date falls, namely the pay period containing 5 April each year, in accordance with regulation 1(2).

Regulation 6 – Meaning of "hourly rate of pay"

6 Meaning of "hourly rate of pay"

(1) The "hourly rate of pay", in relation to a relevant employee, is to be determined as follows—

Step 1

Identify all amounts of ordinary pay and bonus pay paid to the employee during the relevant pay period.

Step 2

Where an amount identified under Step 1 is an amount of ordinary pay, exclude any amount that would normally fall to be paid in a different pay period.

Step 3

Where an amount identified under Step 1 is an amount of bonus pay, and is paid in respect of a period ("the bonus period") which is not the same length as the relevant pay period, divide the amount by the length of the bonus period (in days) and multiply it by the length of the relevant pay period (in days).

Step 4

Add together the amounts identified under Step 1 (as adjusted, where necessary, under Steps 2 and 3).

Step 5

Multiply the amount found under Step 4 by the appropriate multiplier (see paragraphs (2) and (3)).

Step 6

Divide the amount found under Step 5 by the number of working hours in a week for that employee (see regulation 7).

(2) In this regulation, "the appropriate multiplier" means 7 divided by the number of days in the relevant pay period.

(3) In determining for the purposes of this regulation the number of days in the relevant pay period or bonus period where those periods are (or are determined by reference to) a month or a year —

(a) a month is treated as having 30.44 days;

(b) a year is treated as having 365.25 days.

The definition of "hourly rate of pay" is set out in Regulation 6, with step-by-step instructions for working it out. To determine the hourly rate of pay, the employer must first identify all amounts of ordinary pay and bonus pay paid to the employee during the relevant pay period. Any amount of ordinary pay identified as paid during the relevant period is then disregarded, if it would normally fall to be paid during a different pay period. In other words, the Regulations require employers to assess only the pay which the employee actually became entitled to receive during the relevant pay period. For example, any arrears of pay to which the employee had first become entitled to receive during a different pay period, or any mistaken overpayment, would not be included.

Next, the employer looks at bonus pay which was identified as paid during the relevant pay period. If the bonus pay was paid in respect of a period which is not the same length as the relevant pay period, then the amount of bonus must be divided by the length of the bonus period in days and multiplied by the length of the relevant pay period in days. This gives a notional sum representing how much of the bonus pay the employee was paid during the relevant pay period. For example, where the relevant pay period is the month in which 5 April falls, but bonus is paid in that month which relates to the previous year's performance, the bonus pay used in the calculation will be the bonus pay divided by 365, then multiplied by 30.44 representing April.

Next, the employer adds up the ordinary pay figure and the calculated bonus pay figure to give a figure representing what the employee earned during the relevant pay period. Then, that sum is multiplied by the appropriate multiplier. The appropriate multiplier is found by dividing the ordinary and bonus pay received by the employee in the relevant pay period by the number of days in the relevant pay period, and multiplying by seven. This gives a figure representing what that employee earnt each week at the time. Where the relevant pay period or bonus period calculation is determined by reference to a month or a year, a month is treated as having 30.44 days in it, and a year is treated as having 365.25 days in it. Finally, the total sum is divided by the number of working hours in a week for the employee that week, to give a figure representing what that employee was earning per hour during the relevant pay period.

The ACAS/GEO Guidance contains this example:

> For Example... Jenny, a full-pay relevant employee, received £300 in bonus and £1000 in ordinary pay for the period involving the snapshot date. This makes a total of £1300. Jenny has a pay period of 14 days, so the calculation needed would be 7 divided by 14, making the appropriate multiplier 0.5. £1300 multiplied by 0.5 brings the amount to £650. Jenny has weekly working

> hours of 40 hours per week, so the calculation needed would be £650 divided by 40, making the hourly pay £16.25.

The calculations are:

£300 + £1000 = £1300

£1,300 x (7 / 14) = £650

£650 / 40 = £16.25

An example of calculating the correct fraction of bonus which an employee earns during the relevant pay period is given later in the ACAS/GEO Guidance:

> For example... bonus pay recalculation when calculating hourly pay
>
> Gregor, a full-pay relevant employee, is paid on a monthly basis but he also received a bonus payment of £2300 in the pay period that included the snapshot date. The bonus period actually covered three months – the same duration as the last three pay periods in total (including the one with the snapshot date).
>
> - The pay period amounts to 30.44 days (1 month)
> - The bonus period amounts to 91.32 days (3 months)
>
> To work out how much of this bonus relates to the relevant pay period, his employer needs to divide the £2300 by 91.32 – giving a figure of £25.19. They then need to multiply this figure by 30.44 – giving a result of £776.79 (sic) bonus payment relevant to the pay period in question.
>
> Note – this example works through the steps and rounds up the figures to the nearest penny. Employers may choose to calculate more accurately.

Here are the sums to work out the correct fraction of his bonus pay which Gregor received in the relevant pay period which included 5 April:

Step 1

Gregor received bonus pay of £2300 as well as ordinary pay during the relevant pay period.

Step 3

Gregor's bonus pay period is three months, not his ordinary pay period of one month. Under Regulation 6(3)(a), one month is treated as 30.44 days. Therefore, three months is treated as 30.44 days x 3 = 91.32 days. Gregor's bonus pay during the relevant pay period is therefore (£2300 / 91.32) x 30.44 = £25.186 x 30.44 = £766.67 (to the nearest penny).

Regulation 7 – Employee's working hours in a week

7 Employee's working hours in a week

(1) The number of working hours in a week for a relevant employee, for the purposes of Step 6 in regulation 6, is to be determined as follows.

(2) Subject to paragraph (6), where an employee has normal working hours that do not differ from week to week or over a longer period, the number of working hours in a week for a relevant employee is the number of the normal working hours in a week for that employee under the employee's contract of employment, or terms of employment, in force on the snapshot date.

(3) Subject to paragraph (6), where the employee has no normal working hours, or the number of the normal working hours differs from week to week or over a longer period, the number of working hours in a week for the employee is—

(a) the average number of working hours calculated by dividing by twelve the total number of the employee's working hours during the period of twelve weeks ending with the last complete week of the relevant pay period, or

(b) where the employee has not been at work for a sufficient period, or for some other reason the employer is not reasonably able to make the calculation under paragraph (a), a number which fairly represents the number of working hours in a week having regard to such of the considerations specified in paragraph (5) as are appropriate in the circumstances.

(4) In calculating the average number of working hours for the purposes of paragraph (3)(a), no account is to be taken of a week in which no hours were worked by the employee, and hours worked in earlier weeks must be brought in so as to bring up to twelve the number of weeks of which account is taken.

(5) The considerations referred to in paragraph (3)(b) are—

(a) the average number of working hours in a week which the employee could expect under the employee's contract of employment, or terms of employment; and

(b) the average number of working hours of other employees engaged in comparable employment with the same employer.

(6) Where the employee is paid on the basis of piecework, the number of working hours in a week for the employee is the number of hours of output work for that employee in the week during the relevant pay period within which the snapshot date falls, determined in accordance with Chapter 4 of Part 5 of the National Minimum Wage Regulations 2015.

(7) In its application by virtue of paragraph (6), Chapter 4 of Part 5 of the National Minimum Wage Regulations 2015 has effect as if—

(a) references to a worker were references to an employee, and

(b) references to a pay reference period were references to a week.

(8) In this regulation, "working hours"—

(a) includes hours when an employee is available, and required to be available, at or near a place of work for the purposes of working unless the employee is at home, and

(b) excludes any hours for which an employee is entitled to overtime pay.

(9) In paragraph (8), hours when a worker is "available" only includes hours when the worker is awake for the purposes of working, even if a worker by arrangement sleeps at or near a place of work and the employer provides suitable facilities for sleeping.

Regulation 7 explains how to calculate an employee's working hours in a week.

If the employee has normal working hours which do not differ from week to week or over a longer period, then the number of working hours in a week for the relevant employee is the number of normal working hours in a week for the employee under the contract of employment or terms of employment (for example, under a collective agreement) in force on the snapshot date.

If the employee has no normal working hours, or the number of normal working hours differs from week to week or over a longer period (for example, term-time working for school lunchtime meal assistants, school teachers, or university lecturers), the number of working hours in a week for that employee is either the average number of working hours calculated by dividing by 12 the total number of the employee's working hours during the 12-week period ending with the last complete week of the relevant pay period or, if the employee has not been at work for a sufficient period of time or for some other reason the employer is not reasonably able to make the calculation, a number which "fairly represents" the number of working hours in a week having regard to such specific considerations as are appropriate in the circumstances.

When calculating the average number of working hours in the 12-week period, no account is to be taken of a week in which no hours were worked by the employee (for example, when the employee was off sick, on holiday or absent on maternity leave) and therefore hours worked in earlier weeks must be brought in so as to bring up to 12 the number of weeks of which account is taken. For example, if the employee had a week off for his child's half term school holiday during the 12-week period, then the employer should ignore that week and instead use the working hours from the week immediately before the 12-week period. The specific considerations which apply – if the employer decides that it is not reasonable to calculate the working hours and instead a number should be picked to "fairly represent" the employee's working hours - are: the average number of working hours in a week which the employee could expect under the employee's contract of employment or terms of employment; and the average number of working hours of other employees engaged in comparable employment with the same employer.

If the employee is employed on the basis of piecework, then the number of working hours in the week for the employee is the number of hours of output work for that employee in a week during the relevant pay period within which 5 April falls, determined in accordance with Chapter 4 of Part 5 of the National Minimum Wage Regulations 2015. The National Minimum Wage Regulations 2015 have effect as if references there to "worker" were to "employee" and references to "pay reference period" were references to "a week".

For the purposes of regulation 7, "working hours" includes hours when an employee is available and required to be available at or near a place of work for the purposes of working unless the employee is at home and it excludes any hours for which an employee is entitled to overtime pay. The concept of "available" only includes hours when the worker (sic) is awake for the purposes of working, even if a worker by arrangement sleeps at or near a place of work and the employer provides suitable facilities for sleeping.

Regulation 7 gives employers a very broad discretion to calculate "working hours" as they see fit. In the British labour market in general, men dominate the most senior and managerial roles in most organisations, which tend to be the highest-paid jobs. As women tend to be in the minority in the highest-paid roles and also to be more junior within the hierarchies of senior employees in most organisations, it is an obvious temptation for employers to overstate the number of hours which the highest-paid men in the organisation work, in order to bring down the figure which represents the sum which such men are earning each hour.

No doubt for this reason, the Law Society in its guidance to solicitors on gender pay gap reporting[9] advises firms to use for partners the same weekly working hours used for employees, which is typically 35, 37.5 or 40 hours a week. This reflects the fact the UK opted out of the 48-hour cap on working hours contained in the European Union Working Time Directive[10] and it is commonplace for many British workers to work in excess of 48 hours a week. Many solicitors whose contracts of employment state a lower number of hours each week, such as 35, 37.5 or 40 hours, some of whom have signed a personal opt-out to the 48-hour week cap on working hours, in practice regularly work long hours in excess of 40 and indeed in excess of 48: it is not just partners, senior managers or the highest-paid solicitors who work long hours in Britain.

Indeed, if it is the case that the best-paid employees in an organisation are senior men who work excessively long hours above 35, 37.5, 40 or 48 hours a week, the exercise of producing the gender pay gap figures may prompt employers to reflect on why they have not recruited or retained sufficient numbers of women in those roles, and what impact the excessively long hours of work are having on the health, welfare,

9 Law Society, "Gender pay gap reporting: Setting the standard for the Profession", 6 November 2018, https://www.lawsociety.org.uk/support-services/advice/articles/gender-pay-gap-reporting-setting-the-standard/

10 Directive of the European Parliament and of the Council, 4 November 2003, 2003/88/EC

capacity to avoid burnout from the workforce, and ability to participate in family life of their most senior and highly-skilled men.

The significance of the employer's choices about how to approach calculating an employee's working hours in a week is shown by the fact that the ACAS/GEO Guidance gives five examples.

Tania is used as an example of a newly-hired relevant employee whose working pattern has yet to be established:

> For example... less than 12 weeks employment
>
> Tania has been hired for a newly created role and it isn't clear what the normal working hours will end up being, or if there will even be normal working hours –
>
> so for now her employer has guaranteed a minimum of 15 hours work each week. By the end of the relevant pay period she has been working for 6 weeks and worked 150 hours. Her employer therefore makes an average calculation from the six weeks Tania worked, which is 25 weekly working hours. If Tania had been taking over a more predictable role that someone else had been carrying out before she started, it may have been reasonable to come up with a representative number of hours for Tania based on the average number of working hours of the comparable employee.

Jaz is used as an example of a relevant employee who had an unusually quiet week during the relevant pay period into which the snapshot date fell:

> For example... some other reason Jaz, a full-pay relevant employee with a variable hours contract, is paid weekly under the following contractual terms:
>
> - basic pay of £7.50 per hour
> - an evening shift premium of £2 per hour
> - a productivity allowance of £5 for every 100 items packed

Jaz had a relatively quiet week during the relevant pay period. She worked 25 hours, including one evening shift of 5 hours and packed 400 items. Her pay during the relevant pay period is therefore:

- basic pay of £187.50 (£7.50 x 25 hours)
- an evening shift premium of £10 (£2 x 5 hours)
- a productivity allowance of £20 (for packing 400 items)
- a total payment of £217.50

However, Jaz actually worked significantly more than 25 hours per week over the last 12 weeks. On average (including the week during the relevant pay period), she worked 40 hours a week.

If her employer used the standard calculation outlined in step B earlier in this section of the guide, they would need to divide the £217.50 into 40 hours, giving Jaz an hourly rate of £5.44 an hour. This is clearly unrepresentative because it is lower than even the basic hourly pay rate.

Her employer uses the 'some other reason' provision in the regulations and decides to calculate Jaz's hourly rate of pay by dividing her £217.50 weekly pay during the relevant pay period by the 25 hours actually worked in that period. This calculation provides a more representative hourly rate of £8.70.

Then the ACAS/GEO Guidance gives the example of Jeff, who works on annualised hours:

For example... Minimum annualised hours

Jeff, a teacher...

- is a full-pay relevant employee on the snapshot date.
- is required to work a minimum of 1,265 hours over 39 weeks.

- does not need to have annual leave added separately because his paid hours per week are the same for annual leave and work.

Jeff's employer divides his 1,265 minimum hours by 39 working weeks, which makes his basic weekly hours 32 hours and 26 minutes.

The ACAS/GEO Guidance also gives an example of a full-pay relevant employee who works unspecified hours, Mei:

For example... Unspecified hours

Mei, a head teacher at the same school as Jeff above...

- is a full-pay relevant employee on the snapshot date.
- does not have specified working hours but her work amounts to broadly the same overall amount of work as Jeff in the example above.
- does not need to have annual leave added separately because her paid hours per week are the same for annual leave and work.

Mei's employer records her basic weekly working hours as 32 hours and 26 minutes so meaningful comparisons can be drawn.

The ACAS/GEO Guidance gives an example of a term-time worker called Sam:

For example... Term time workers

Sam...

- is a full-pay relevant employee on the snapshot date
- works 10 hours a week over 39 weeks.
- gets 5 weeks of annual leave, which is taken outside of the 39 weeks
- gets paid in 12 equal instalments no matter how many hours she works that month

Taking a 12 week average of weekly working hours and discounting weeks Sam didn't work is unlikely to represent how her pay and work matches up.

Instead, her employer finds a fair alternative method that represents Sam's average weekly hours...

- They add her 39 work weeks and 5 annual leave weeks, making 44 paid weeks per year. They multiply this by the 10 hours Sam works to get 440 paid hours each year.
- They average out her hours over the whole year, just like the payments are, by dividing her 440 paid hours by 52.18 (the exact number of weeks in a year).

This makes Sam's average weekly hours just under 8½ hours a week and the method works for other full and part time term time workers too.

Finally, the ACAS/GEO Guidance contains a warning to employers that the decision whether or not to include hours worked with on-call or sleeping-in arrangements must be in line with the National Minimum Wages Regulations 2015[11]. This area of law can be complicated and is likely to depend on the specific and unique facts of the case, so the warning is apt.

Regulation 8 – Difference in mean hourly rate of pay

8 Difference in mean hourly rate of pay

The difference between the mean hourly rate of pay of male full-pay relevant employees and that of female full-pay relevant employees must be expressed as a percentage of the mean hourly rate of pay of male full pay relevant employees and is to be determined as follows—

((A - B) / A) x 100

11 SI 2015/621

where—

A is the mean hourly rate of pay of all male full-pay relevant employees; and

B is the mean hourly rate of pay of all female full-pay relevant employees.

Under the Regulation 8, employers must present their gender pay gap figures as percentages. Regulation 8 provides that the difference between the mean hourly rate of male full-pay relevant employees and the mean hourly rate of female full-pay relevant employees must be expressed as a percentage of the mean hourly rate of pay of the male full-pay relevant employees and gives the formula for the calculation.

The ACAS/GEO Guidance gives this example:

> For example... An employer with a mean hourly rate of pay of £15.25 for all male full-pay relevant employees and £13.42 for all female full-pay relevant employees would have a 12.0% mean gender pay gap (rounded to one decimal place).

The calculations are:

A = £15.25

B = £13.42

[(£15.25 - £13.42) / £15.25] x 100 = (£1.83/£15.25) x 100
= 0.12 x 100 = 12

Regulation 9 – Difference in median hourly rate of pay

9 Difference in median hourly rate of pay

The difference between the median hourly rate of pay of male full-pay relevant employees and that of female full-pay relevant employees must be expressed as a percentage of the median pay of

> male full-pay relevant employees and is to be determined as follows—
>
> ((A - B) / A) x 100
>
> where—
>
> A is the median hourly rate of pay of all male full-pay relevant employees; and
>
> B is the median hourly rate of pay of all female full-pay relevant employees.

Regulation 9 explains how to calculate the difference between the median hourly rate of pay of male full-pay relevant employees and the median hourly rate of pay of female full-pay relevant employees as a percentage, using the same basis of calculation as regulation 8. As with the difference between mean pay, the median gender pay gap in pay must be expressed as a percentage of the male pay, on the assumption that in most British workplaces, men are paid more than women.

This example is from the ACAS/GEO Guidance:

> For example…
>
> An employer with a median hourly rate of pay of £16.00 for all male full-pay relevant employees and £13.50 for all female full-pay relevant employees would have a 15.6% median gender pay gap (rounded to one decimal place).

The calculations are:

A = £16.00

B = £13.50

[(£16.00 - £13.50) / £16.00] x 100 = (£2.50 / £16.00) x 100 =

0.15625 x 100 = 15.625 = 15.63 (to one decimal place)

Regulation 10 – Difference in mean bonus pay

> 10 Difference in mean bonus pay
>
> (1) The difference between the mean bonus pay paid to male relevant employees and that paid to female relevant employees must be expressed as a percentage of the mean bonus pay paid to male relevant employees and is to be determined as follows—
>
> ((A - B) / A) x 100
>
> where—
>
> A is the mean bonus pay paid during the relevant period to male relevant employees who were paid bonus pay during that period; and
>
> B is the mean bonus pay paid during the relevant period to female relevant employees who were paid bonus pay during that period.
>
> (2) In this regulation "the relevant period" means the period of 12 months ending with the snapshot date.

Regulation 10 sets out how to calculate the different in mean bonus pay, again using the same formula, which expresses the gender pay gap as a percentage of the bonus pay of the male employees. The difference is between the mean bonus pay paid to male relevant employees who were paid bonus pay during the relevant period and the mean bonus pay paid to female relevant employees who were paid bonus pay during the relevant period. The "relevant period" for the purposes of bonus pay is the period of 12 months ending with 5 April.

This example is from the ACAS/GEO Guidance:

> For example... An employer with a mean bonus pay of £1650 for all male relevant employees and £1490 for all female relevant employees would have a 9.7% mean bonus gender pay gap (rounded to one decimal place).

The calculation is performed like this:

A = £1650

B = £1490

Mean bonus pay gap is [(£1650 - £1490) / £1650] x 100 = (£160 / £1650) x 100

= 0.097 x 100 (to three decimal places) = 9.7 (to one decimal place)

Regulation 11 – Difference in median bonus pay

> 11 Difference in median bonus pay
>
> (1) The difference between the median bonus pay paid to male relevant employees and that paid to female relevant employees must be expressed as a percentage of the median bonus pay paid to male relevant employees and is to be determined as follows—
>
> ((A - B) / A) x 100
>
> where—
>
> A is the median bonus pay paid during the relevant period to male relevant employees who were paid bonus pay during that period; and
>
> B is the median bonus pay paid during the relevant period to female relevant employees who were paid bonus pay during that period.
>
> (2) In this regulation "the relevant period" means the period of 12 months ending with the snapshot date.

Under Regulation 11, the difference in median bonus pay is to be calculated in the same way, as a percentage. The difference between the median bonus pay of male relevant employees who were paid bonus pay during the relevant period and the median bonus pay of female relevant employees who were paid bonus pay during the relevant period must be expressed a percentage of the median bonus pay paid to male relevant employees during the relevant period. Only employees who were paid bonus pay are included and the "relevant period" is the 12 months ending with the snapshot date.

The ACAS/GEO Guidance gives this example, and the calculations are below:

> For example… An employer with a median bonus pay of £2300 for all male relevant employees and £2225 for all female relevant employees would have a 3.3% median bonus gender pay gap (rounded to one decimal place).

Here are the calculations:

A = £2300

B = £2225

Median bonus pay gap is [(£2300 - £2225) / £2300] x 100 = (£75 / £2300) x 100

= 0.033 x 100 (to three decimal places) = 3.3 (to one decimal place)

Regulation 12 – Proportion of male and female employees who received bonus pay

> 12 Proportion of male and female employees who received bonus pay
>
> (1) The proportion of male relevant employees who were paid bonus pay must be expressed as a percentage of male relevant employees and is to be determined as follows—
>
> (A / B) x 100
>
> where—
>
> A is the number of male relevant employees who were paid bonus pay during the relevant period; and
>
> B is the number of male relevant employees.

> (2) The proportion of female relevant employees who were paid bonus pay must be expressed as a percentage of female relevant employees and is to be determined as follows—
>
> (A / B) x 100
>
> where—
>
> A is the number of female relevant employees who were paid bonus pay during the relevant period; and
>
> B is the number of female relevant employees.
>
> (3) In this regulation "the relevant period" means the period of 12 months ending with the snapshot date.

Regulation 12 contains the calculation method for the expressing the proportions of male and female relevant employees who were paid bonus pay. The proportion of men who received a bonus must be expressed as a percentage of all male relevant employees, and the proportion of women who received a bonus must be expressed as a percentage of all female relevant employees. Again, "the relevant period" is 12 months ending with the snapshot date.

The ACAS/GEO Guidance example is set out below with the addition of the calculations:

> For example... An employer has 302 male relevant employees of which 255 received a bonus, and 258 female relevant employees of which 215 received a bonus. This means 84.4% of male relevant employees received a bonus and 83.3% of female relevant employees received a bonus (rounded to one decimal place).

The calculations are made as follows:

For male relevant employees

A = 250

B = 302

The proportion of male relevant employees who were paid bonus pay is

(255 / 302) x 100 = 0.844 (to three decimal places) x 100 = 84.4% (to one decimal place)

For female relevant employees

A = 215

B = 258

The proportion of female relevant employees who were paid bonus pay is

(215/258) x 100 = 0.833 (to three decimal places) x 100 = 83.3% (to one decimal place)

Regulation 13 – Proportion of male and female employees according to quartile bands

> 13 Proportion of male and female employees according to quartile pay bands
>
> (1) The proportions of male and female full-pay relevant employees in the lower, lower middle, upper middle and upper quartile pay bands is to be determined as follows.
>
> Step 1
>
> Determine the hourly rate of pay for each male and female full-pay relevant employee and then rank those employees in order from lowest paid to highest paid.
>
> Step 2
>
> Divide the employees, as ranked under Step 1, into four sections, each comprising (so far as possible) an equal number of employees, to determine the lower, lower middle, upper middle and upper quartile pay bands.

> Step 3
>
> The proportion of male full-pay relevant employees within each quartile pay band must be expressed as a percentage of the full-pay relevant employees within that band as follows—
>
> (A / B) x 100
>
> where—
>
> A is the number of male full-pay relevant employees in a quartile pay band; and
>
> B is the number of full-pay relevant employees in that quartile pay band.
>
> Step 4
>
> The proportion of female full-pay relevant employees within each quartile pay band must be expressed as a percentage of the full-pay relevant employees within that band as follows—
>
> (A / B) x 100
>
> where—
>
> A is the number of female full-pay relevant employees in a quartile pay band; and
>
> B is the number of full-pay relevant employees in that quartile pay band.
>
> (2) Where employees receiving the same hourly rate of pay fall within more than one quartile pay band, the employer must (so far as possible) ensure that, when ranking the employees under Step 1, the relative proportion of male and female employees receiving that rate of pay is the same in each of those pay bands.

Regulation 13 deals with the quartile bands. Under regulation 13(1), the proportions of male and female full-pay relevant employees in the lower, lower middle, upper middle and upper quartile pay bands must be worked out as follows. First of all, the employer must work out the hourly rate of pay for each male and each female full-pay relevant employee in the workforce, and then rank them in order from the lower paid to the highest paid. Next, the employees must be divided into four equal quarters, to determine the lower, lower middle, upper middle and upper quartile bands. Then, the employer must express the proportion of male full-pay relevant employees within each quartile pay band as a percentage of the full-pay relevant employees within each band. This is done by dividing the number of male full-pay relevant employees within each quartile band by the number of full-pay relevant employees of both sexes within that quartile band, and multiplying by 100. Then, the same calculation is done to obtain the proportion of female full-pay relevant employees within each quartile band, which is also to be expressed as a percentage.

On the basis that in English equal pay law, only two sexes, male and female, are legally recognised, and the Regulations are silent about non-binary relevant employees, nearly all employers should, in my view, end up with calculations in which the percentage of female relevant employees and the percentage of male relevant employees in each quartile add up to 100%. The ACAS/GEO Guidance stresses the importance of "being sensitive to how an employee chooses to self-identify in terms of their gender", since the Regulations do not define the terms "male" and "female"; employers are advised not to ask intrusive personal questions but to base gender pay gap reports on existing information which the employee has provided to payroll, provided the records are up-to-date. For situations in which the payroll information is not available or may be unreliable, ACAS have provided a free template of a communication which employers may send to employees inviting them to check and update their recorded gender. Where an employee does not self-identify to a binary division of gender, the ACAS/GEO Guidance is that an employer may omit that particular employee from the gender pay gap calculations.

Under regulation 13(2), where employees receiving the same hourly rate of pay fall within more than one quartile band (which could happen, for example, in a workforce where a large proportion of employees are receiving hourly rate of pay within a narrow range), then the employer must ensure that, when ranking the employees under Step 1, the relative proportions of male and female employees receiving that rate of pay is the same in each of those pay bands. This is to stop employers giving misleading information about their workforce, for example, by placing all the female employees in a higher quartile than the men, to give a false impression that women in its workforce are employed in more senior or better-paid roles, when in fact that set of male and female full-pay relevant employees are all receiving the same range of hourly pay.

Without any robust Government audit of gender pay gap reporting by employers, however, it is highly likely that many accidental or deliberate errors by employers when placing employees within the quartile bands will remain undetected, particularly where the distortions do not create statistically-improbable errors.

The ACAS/GEO Guidance gives these examples:

> For example... An employer has 322 full-pay relevant employees and has arranged them by lowest hourly rate of pay to the highest hourly rate of pay. They realise that an equal split of employees means 80 employees in each quartile, with 2 employees left over. To distribute the numbers as evenly as possible, they add 1 employee to the lower quartile, and 1 employee to the upper middle quartile. This means there are 81 employees in the lower quartile, 80 employees in the lower middle quartile, 81 employees in the upper middle quartile, and 80 employees in the upper quartile pay bands
>
> For example... An employer has 322 full-pay relevant employees, has arranged them by lowest hourly rate of pay to the highest hourly rate of pay, and has then divided the list into four quartiles. However, 40 staff all have the same hourly rate of pay. 36 are female and 4 are male. Of them, 10 have fallen into the lower quartile, while 30 have fallen into the lower middle quartile. To evenly distribute these staff by gender, the employer

> can see that this means for every 9 females listed, 1 male should be listed with them. Therefore, the employer lists 9 of the female employees and 1 male employee in the lower quartile, and 27 of the female employees and 3 male employees in the lower middle quartile.

The calculations here are:

40 is split by gender 36 : 4 = 9 : 1

40 is split across two quartiles in the ratio 10 : 30 = 1: 3 = (9 + 1) : [3 x (9 + 1)]

The ACAS/GEO Guidance also gives an example of the proportions of male and female employees in each quartile band:

> For example... An employer has 322 full-pay relevant employees, has arranged them by lowest hourly rate of pay to the highest hourly rate of pay, has divided the list into four quartiles and ensured employees on the same hourly pay rate are distributed evenly by gender where they cross the quartile boundaries.
>
> Of the 81 employees in the lower quartile, 48 are male and 33 are female. This means 59.3% are male and 40.7% are female.
>
> Of the 80 employees in the lower middle quartile, 28 are male and 52 are female. This means 35% are male and 65% are female.
>
> Of the 81 employees in the upper middle quartile, 40 are male and 41 are female. This means 49.4% are male and 50.6% are female.
>
> Of the 80 employees in the upper quartile, 58 are male and 22 are female. This means 72.5% are male and 27.5% are female.

Here are the calculations:

Lower Quartile

For the male employees

A = 48

B = 81

The proportion of male employees is (48 / 81) x 100 = 0.593 (to three decimal places) x 100

= 59.3 (to one decimal place) ie 59.3% in the lower quartile band are male

For the female employees

A = 33

B = 81

The proportion of female employees is (33 / 81) x 100 = 0.407 (to three decimal places) x 100

= 40.7 (to one decimal place) ie 40.7% in the lower quartile band are female.

Lower Middle Quartile

For the male employees

A = 28

B = 80

The proportion of male employees is (28 / 80) x 100 = 0.35 x 100 = 35 (to one decimal place) ie 35% in the lower middle quartile band are male.

For the female employees

A = 52

B = 80

The proportion of female employees is (52 / 80) x 100 = 0.65 x 100 = 65.0 (to one decimal place) ie 65% in the lower middle quartile band are female.

Upper Middle Quartile

For the male employees

A = 40

B = 81

The proportion of male employees is (40 / 81) x 100 = 0.494 (to three decimal places) x 100

= 49.4 (to one decimal place) ie 49.4% in the upper middle quartile are male.

For the female employees

A = 41

B = 81

The proportion of female employees is (41 / 81) x 100 = 0.506 (to three decimal places) x 100

= 50.6 (to one decimal place) ie 50.6% in the upper middle quartile are female.

Upper Quartile

For the male employees

A = 58

B = 80

The proportion of male employees is (58 / 80) x 100 = 0.725 x 100 = 72.5 ie 72.5% in the upper quartile are male.

For the female employees

A = 22

B = 80

The proportion of female employees is (22 / 80) x 100 = 0.275 x 100 = 27.5 ie 27.5% in the upper quartile are female.

Regulation 14 – Information to be accompanied by signed statement

14 Information to be accompanied by signed statement

(1) The information published under regulation 2 must be accompanied by a written statement which—

(a) confirms that the information is accurate; and

(b) is signed in accordance with paragraph (2).

(2) Where the relevant employer is—

(a) a body corporate other than a limited liability partnership within the meaning of the Limited Liability Partnerships Act 2000, the written statement must be signed by a director (or equivalent);

(b) a limited liability partnership, the written statement must be signed by a designated member (see section 8 of that Act);

(c) the partners in a limited partnership registered under the Limited Partnerships Act 1907, the written statement must be signed by a general partner (see section 3 of that Act);

(d) the partners in any other kind of partnership, the written statement must be signed by a partner;

(e) the members or officers of an unincorporated body of persons other than a partnership, the written statement must be signed by a member of the governing body or a senior officer;

(f) any other type of body, the written statement must be signed by the most senior employee.

(3) In this regulation, "partnership" means—

(a) a partnership within the Partnership Act 1890;

(b) a limited partnership registered under the Limited Partnerships Act 1907; or

(c) a firm, or an entity of a similar character, formed under the law of a country outside the United Kingdom.

Regulation 14 imposes a duty on a responsible and senior person within the employer's organisation to sign a written statement accompanying the information published by the employer on its gender pay gap in accordance with Regulation 2. The written statement must confirm the accuracy of the information and be signed by a person with a specific status.

For a body corporate other than a limited liability partnership within the meaning of the Limited Liability Partnership Act 2000, the signatory must be a director or equivalent. For a limited liability partnership, it must be signed by a designated member under section 8 of the Limited Liability Partnership Act 2000. A general partner must sign for the partners in a limited partnership registered under the Limited Partnerships Act 1907. The partners under any kind of other partnership must have one partner sign. The members and officers of an unincorporated body of persons other than a partnership must ask a member of the governing body or a senior offer to be signatory, and any other type of body must use "the most senior employee" as their signatory. "Partnership" means a partnership within the Partnership Act 1890, a limited partnership registered under the Limited Partnerships Act 1907 or a firm, or entity of a similar character, formed under the law of a country outside the UK.

Anecdotal evidence suggests that many employers are in breach of the requirements imposed by Regulation 14, because the wrong person, such as a junior clerical assistant or an external payroll consultant, signed off the gender pay gap reporting figures. The requirement to have a very senior person sign off the gender pay gap reporting figures was presumably introduced by Parliament in order to ensure that issues of gender pay gap, pay equality and equal opportunities for female employees received attention at the highest levels within the organisation. Nevertheless, as things stand, and as with so many significant aspects of the Regulations, in practice (apart from the case of major businesses which attract the scrutiny of the financial press) such errors are unlikely to be spotted by anyone, let alone to lead to legal action against the employer, because of the lack of effective enforcement mechanisms in the Regulations.

There is no legal requirement to provide any supportive narrative to the gender pay gap figures.

Nevertheless, the ACAS/GEO Guidance advises the inclusion of a supporting narrative as a matter of best practice:

> All employers should add a supporting narrative – a gender pay gap does not necessarily mean they have acted inappropriately or discriminatorily but this will need explaining.
>
> A narrative helps anyone reading the statement to understand the organisation's view of why a gender pay gap is present and what the organisation intends to do to close it.
>
> An organisation should consider publishing an action plan that explains how it intends to tackle its gender pay gap – a plan with targets and clear actions sends a strong signal of commitment to gender equality in the workplace. An action plan can either be published as part of a supporting narrative or alongside it.

Regulation 15 – Form and manner of publication

> 15 Form and manner of publication
>
> (1) The requirement in regulation 2 to publish information, and the requirement in regulation 14 for the information to be accompanied by a written statement, are requirements that that information and statement be published on the employer's website—
>
> (a) in a manner that is accessible to all its employees and to the public; and
>
> (b) for a period of at least three years beginning with the date of publication.

> (2) A relevant employer must also publish on a website designated for that purpose by the Secretary of State—
>
> (a) the information required by regulation 2, and
>
> (b) the name and job title of the person who signed the statement required by regulation 14.

Under Regulation 15, the employer must publish the gender pay gap information required by Regulation 2 and the written statement required by Regulation 14 on the employer's website, in a way which makes it accessible to all its employees and to the public, for a period of at least three years from the date of publication. It must also be published on the Government website, which has now been set up at https://gender-pay-gap-service.gov.uk.

Aiming to promote best practice, the ACAS/GEO Guidance advises employers that they may enhance their reports into a fuller gender pay gap audit "on a voluntary basis where they consider this informative and appropriate", by supplying additional information in the voluntary narrative which accompanies the gender pay gap information required by law to be published.

Similarly, the ACAS/GEO Guidance says:

> Employers should add gender pay reporting into a sensible point of their reporting cycle but aim to publish their results as soon after the snapshot date as is reasonable for them to do. There are practical advantages to this:
>
> - Those who publish earliest can be seen as leaders/exemplar in their sector and gain from brand and reputation enhancement, e.g. positive impacts on recruitment, retention and contract awards.
> - It's easier to work with fresh data that is more readily recalled than trying to unearth old data that may have been archived and is harder to access.

- An employer can avoid planning to publish at the last minute only to find that key employees are on sick leave or there are other unplanned absences.
- Unanticipated issues or complications can be tackled earlier on.
- Early analysis and publication encourages early action to tackle any pay gaps identified.

Regulation 16 – Review

16 Review

(1) The Secretary of State must from time to time—

(a) carry out a review of these Regulations;

(b) set out the conclusion of the review in a report; and

(c) publish the report.

(2) The report must in particular—

(a) set out the objectives intended to be achieved by these Regulations;

(b) assess the extent to which those objectives are achieved; and

(c) assess whether those objectives remain appropriate and, if so, the extent to which they could be achieved with a system that imposes less regulation.

(3) The first report under this regulation must be published before the end of the period of five years beginning with the day on which these Regulations come into force.

(4) Reports under this regulation are afterwards to be published at intervals not exceeding five years.

Regulation 16 provides that the Secretary of State must carry out a review of the Regulations, produce a report with conclusions, and publish it. The first report, however, will not be due until 5 April 2022 and then at intervals not exceeding five years.

The report must set out the objectives intended to be achieved by the Regulations, assess the extent to which those objectives are achieved, and assess whether those objectives remain appropriate and, if so, the extent to which they could be achieved with a system that imposed less regulation.

It can be seen, therefore, that the Regulations contain no enforcement mechanisms, apart from whatever public relations concerns may arise from the duty to publish the gender pay gap information in a way which an employer's own employees and the general public may see, and the pre-existing role of the EHRC. The financial publications, in particular, have kept an eye on the gender pay gap figures of the largest companies, however, many medium-sized companies are of little interest to the press.

It is also interesting that, rather than stating the objectives of the Regulations in the Regulations themselves, at the outset, Regulation 16(2)(a) leaves it for whoever is the Secretary of State on or around 5 April 2022 to decide with hindsight and with a political perspective what the objectives were and whether they have been met.

The Regulations constitute the first attempt to require employers in Britain to present the gender pay gap in their workforce for public scrutiny. To that extent, the Regulations are an important step forward towards the goal of enforcing British women's right to equal pay for equal work in the Equality Act 2010. In my opinion, the Regulations have not moved further than the longstanding objective of the "Think, Act, Report" scheme which preceded them, however, they may finally have achieved that limited objective, which the voluntary scheme never did.

CHAPTER EIGHT
THE ROLE OF THE EQUALITY AND HUMAN RIGHTS COMMISSION

Summary: In this chapter, I consider the duties and powers of the Equality and Human Rights Commission, its Statutory Code of Practice on Equal Pay, its Five Step Equal Pay Audit Model, its enforcement policy, and its Report on the 2018 gender pay gap reporting cycle.

Duties and Powers of the Equality and Human Rights Commission

The EHRC was established by the Equality Act 2006 and has the general duty under section 3:

> 3 General duty
>
> The Commission shall exercise its functions under this Part with a view to encouraging and supporting the development of a society in which –
>
> (a) people's ability to achieve their potential is not limited by prejudice or discrimination,
>
> (b) there is respect for and protection of each individual's human rights,
>
> (c) there is respect for the dignity and worth of each individual,
>
> (d) each individual has an equal opportunity to participate in society; and
>
> (e) there is mutual respect between groups based on understanding and valuing of diversity and on shared respect or equality and human rights.

The EHRC has specific duties to promote equality and diversity, under section 8, and human rights, under section 9.

The EHRC has a range of enforcement powers associated with its duties under the Equality Act 2006. It may:

(i) conduct inquiries into equality and diversity and human rights matters (section 16);

(ii) investigate a breach of equality and human rights law, or of unlawful act notices or undertakings made under the Equality Act 2006 (section 20);

(iii) give a person notice that he or she has committed an unlawful act, require preparation of an action plan, or recommend action (section 21);

(iv) enter to an agreement with a person who undertakes not to commit an unlawful act, or to take or refrain from specified action (section 23);

(v) apply to court for an injunction restraining a person from committing an unlawful act (section 24);

(vi) give legal assistance to an individual who is or may become party to legal proceedings (section 28);

(vii) institute or intervene in legal proceedings (section 30);

(viii) assess the extent to which a public authority has complied with the public sector equality duty (section 31); and

(ix) issue a notice of failure to comply with the public sector equality duty (section 32).

It follows that the EHRC is empowered to carry out inquiries into the extent and causes of pay gaps in particular sectors or areas, and conduct investigations of any employer which it suspects of having unlawfully discriminatory pay practices or of failing to comply with the Regulations. If the EHRC were to conduct an investigation or inquiry, it could require an employer to provide it with information, documents and oral evidence about its pay policies or practices[1]. The employer would have to provide the pay information, unless the request from the EHRC were unnecessary given the purpose of the inquiry or investigation, or otherwise unreasonable.

On the other hand, the enforcement of British female employees' rights to equal pay and to a workplace free from unlawful sex discrimination is just one of the EHRC's many concerns. In 2009, the EHRC used its powers to inquire into pay gaps between men and women in the financial services sector[2], but since then it does not appear to have investigated pay equality or gender pay gaps in any other area of the labour market. On 12 March 2019, the EHRC announced its intention to conduct an investigation into pay practices at the British Broadcasting Corporation[3]. In terms of court interventions, in 2009, the EHRC intervened at Court of Appeal level in an equal pay case, and in 2011, the EHRC intervened in an Employment Tribunal case on equal pay[4]. The EHRC produced its Statutory Code of Practice on Equal Pay in 2011[5].

---

1 See further the Equality Act 2006, Schedule 2 Inquiries, Investigations and Assessments

2 Equality and Human Rights Commission, "Financial Services Inquiry, Sex Discrimination and Gender Pay Gap", 1 September 2009, https://www.equalityhumanrights.com/sites/default/files/financial_services_inquiry_report_0.pdf

3 Maya Oppenheim, "BBC equal pay row to be investigated by Equality and Human Rights Commission", Independent, 12 March 2019, https://www.independent.co.uk/news/uk/home-news/bbc-equal-pay-women-investigation-ehrc-a8818971.html

4 Equality and Human Rights Commission, "Summary of commission interventions concluded", 4 May 2018, https://www.equalityhumanrights.com/sites/default/files/summary-of-commission-interventions-concluded.xlsx

5 https://www.equalityhumanrights.com/sites/default/files/equalpaycode.pdf

As part of wide-ranging and deep austerity cuts made to state services after the 2008 global financial crisis, in 2016 the budget of the EHRC was set to plummet from £62 million in 2010 to £17.4 million in 2020, which commentators predicted would leave it as a toothless watchdog[6]. For 2018-2019, the EHRC's budget is £19.47m[7]. The EHRC operates a telephone helpline offering free information about the Equality Act 2010 and provides some information on its website about equal pay and gender pay gap reporting. It has also produced an enforcement policy for gender pay gap reporting, entered into correspondence with some employers, and published a written Report on the 2018 gender pay gap reporting cycle.

The Statutory Code of Practice on Equal Pay

In January 2011, the EHRC issued a Statutory Code of Practice on Equal Pay under section 14 of the Equality Act 2006. It does not create any new legal obligations, but it is intended to provide authoritative statutory guidance on interpreting the Equality Act 2010, including the equal pay rules. The statutory code has not been updated by the EHRC to mention that section 78 of the Equality Act 2010 was brought into force and the Regulations were made.

The Chair of the EHRC set out in 2011 in the Statutory Code the EHRC's attitude towards enforcement action:

> The Equality and Human Rights Commission has a key role to pay in bringing the [Equality] Act [2010] to life. We have a powerful set of tools to enforce the law. We can, for example,

6 Jamie Doward, The Observer, "Equality watchdog's human rights fight 'under threat' after cuts", 20 November 2016, https://www.theguardian.com/society/2016/nov/20/equality-human-rights-commission-cuts-under-threat

7 Equality and Human Rights Commission, "Business Plan 2018/19", March 2018, https://www.equalityhumanrights.com/sites/default/files/business-plan-2018-2019.pdf

> take organisations to court and intervene in individual discrimination cases. But we only want to intervene when things go wrong as a last resort. Our first priority is to provide information, support and encouragement so that organisations can get it right in the first place.

The second part of the EHRC's Statutory Code is called "Good equal pay practice." According to the EHRC:

> Pay is one of the key factors affecting motivation and relationships at work. It is therefore important to develop pay arrangements that are right for the organisation and that reward employees fairly. Providing equal pay for equal work is central to the concept of rewarding people fairly for what they do.

The EHRC recommends that all employers should carry out regular equal pay audits because that is "the most effective way of establishing whether an organisation is in fact providing equal pay" for equal work. It considers that conducting an equal pay audit "demonstrates appropriate action to identify and eliminate gender pay discrimination" and that an equal pay audit "provides a risk assessment tool for pay structures".

It says:

> A number of common pay practices, listed below, pose risks in terms of potential non-compliance with an employer's legal obligations:
>
> - lack of transparency and unnecessary secrecy over grading and pay
> - discretionary pay systems (for example, merit pay and performance-related pay) unless they are clearly structured and based on objective criteria

- different non-basic pay, terms and conditions for different groups of employees (for example, attendance allowances, overtime or unsocial hours payments)
- more than one grading and pay system within the organisation
- long pay scales or salary ranges
- overlapping pay scales or ranges, where the maximum of the lower pay scale is higher than the minimum of the next higher scale, including 'broad-banded' structures where there are significant overlaps
- managerial discretion over starting salaries
- market-based pay systems or supplements not underpinned by job evaluation
- job evaluation systems which have been incorrectly implemented or not kept up to date
- pay protection policies

The Statutory Code recommends that employers conduct an equal pay audit not just to reduce the risk of having to defend costly equal pay litigation, but because it offers benefits to the organisation, including identifying, explaining and, where unjustifiable, eliminating pay inequalities; having rational, fair and transparent pay arrangements; demonstrating to employees and to potential employees a commitment to equality; and demonstrating the organisation's values to those with whom it does business.

An equal pay audit is defined by the EHRC as an exercise involving comparing the pay of men and women who are doing equal work in an organisation, identifying and explaining any pay differences and eliminating pay inequalities which cannot be explained on non-discriminatory grounds. It stresses that an equal pay audit goes beyond collecting gender pay gap data:

An equal pay audit is not simply a data collection exercise. It entails a commitment to put right any unjustified pay inequalities. This means that the audit must have the involvement and support of managers who have the authority to deliver the necessary changes.

The validity of the audit and the success of subsequent action taken will be enhanced if the pay system is understood and accepted by the managers who operate the system, by the employees and by their unions. Employers should therefore aim to secure the involvement of employees and, where possible, trade union and other employee representatives, when carrying out an equal pay audit.

The Five Step Equal Pay Audit Model

The EHRC recommends a five-step equal pay audit model:

Step 1: Decide the scope of the audit and identify the information required

Step 2: Determine where men and women are doing equal work

Step 3: Collect and compare pay data to identify any significant pay inequalities between roles of equal value

Step 4: Establish the causes of any significant pay inequalities and assess the reasons for them

Step 5: Develop an equal pay action plan to remedy any direct or indirect pay discrimination

The first step involves deciding the scope of the audit and identifying the information required. Employers will be asking themselves which employees they are going to include, what information they need and what tools are available, what resources are required, who should be involved in conducting the audit, when the workforce should be involved, and whether expert advice is needed.

I think that a key question for any employer must be whether to limit the equal pay audit to pay differences between men and women, simply because that is what the Regulations require, or whether the employer will find it more useful to include intersections of inequality, by also auditing pay differences associated with pregnancy and maternity, parenthood, marital or family status, race, disability, sexual orientation, religion, gender identity, age, educational or training background, socio-economic origins, or other personal characteristics.

Similarly, depending on the nature of the workforce, the employer may also have to make significant choices about which sets of workers to include. For example, a law firm may decide to include equity partners within its equal pay audit, in accordance with Law Society advice[8], even though they are not strictly speaking covered by the gender pay gap reporting requirements in the Regulations, because becoming an equity partner is the aspiration of many junior solicitors and the firm would like to take action to increase the numbers of women partners. For another employer, it might make practical sense to include casual workers or agency workers within the scope of its equal pay audit, whether or not as a matter of law they fall within the definition of "employee", because of the way its business operates, and not to limit the equal pay audit to the requirements of the Regulations.

The most effective equal pay audits involve stakeholders from different areas of the organisation, typically: the managers responsible for pay and grading structures; payroll staff; human resources leaders; any equality, diversity and inclusion team which may exist; individual employees; and trade unions or employee representatives. Depending on the size, resources and existing expertise of the organisation, it may be wise to bring in external expert advice from a reputable professional equal pay

8 Law Society, "Gender pay gap reporting: Setting the standard for the profession", 6 November 2018, https://www.lawsociety.org.uk/support-services/advice/articles/gender-pay-gap-reporting-setting-the-standard/

audit service. Some employers have brought lawyers into the equal pay audit team with the hope of establishing legal professional privilege which could be relied upon to avoid disclosing voluntarily-collected gender pay gap data in any future equal pay litigation. The alternative is deliberately to choose to conduct an equal pay audit which is transparent to the workforce and management, and this is likely to require careful consideration of how to explain the results to the wider internal audience in way which fosters good working relationships.

Given the sensitive and personal nature of pay information and the personal characteristics which most employers would consider relevant to a useful equal pay audit, it is very important to give early consideration to data protection requirements. The Data Protection Act 2018 imposes onerous duties on employers.

At step 2, the employer determines where men and women are doing equal work. Given the complexities of equal pay law, it is unlikely that the employer will be able to establish who is doing equal work without taking expert advice, unless it has recently conducted a professional job evaluation exercise across its workforce.

The third step is to collect and compare pay data to identify any significant pay inequalities between roles which constitute equal work. This requires the calculation of average basic pay and total earnings. As the Law Society advises, for some employers, the approach taken in the Regulations, taking a snapshot pay period which includes 5 April each year, may not be the most informative approach for an employer's own equal pay audit. Another approach, such as comparing total remuneration over a calendar year, may give the employer greater insight into patterns of earnings, motivation, retention and progression across the organisation.

The quality of both the payroll data and the information about the employees' sex and other personal characteristics will be critical to the value of the equal pay audit. Similarly, the choice of software will be extremely important, as this will affect the ease with which the pay data can be collected and analysed. There is currently a wide range of software relevant to gender pay gap reporting available both for employers to buy for themselves and for organisations to access through external specialist providers, and so the choice should be made carefully.

At step 4 of the five-step equal pay audit model, the employer will establish the causes of any significant pay inequalities and assess the reasons for them. Common factors for pay gaps between men and women include length of service, starting salaries which perpetuate pay inequality between men and women in the wider labour market, pay protection schemes, pay progression scales, market factors associated with occupational segregation which values work lower which is stereotypically regarded as women's work, and performance.

Unfortunately, practical experience in equal pay litigation has shown me that employers sometimes discover pay discrepancies which turn out to be caused by genuine mistakes which are embarrassing and awkward to explain to the affected employees, by historic factors which are unknown and hard for the current management to understand, and by direct and indirect sex discrimination. Careful advance consideration should be given as to how the findings of an equal pay audit will be shared with the workforce, including where a large gender pay gap is revealed, and where mistakes, or even unlawful practices, emerge.

Finally, at step 5, the employer should develop an equal pay action plan to remedy any direct or indirect pay discrimination. Pay gaps should be remedied or objectively justified, and, in the meantime, the EHRC recommends introduction of an equal pay policy in the business.

The EHRC also has on its website some information on equal pay audits in general, not just on differences between men and women's pay, and not based on compliance with the Regulations[9]. It is still based

9 Equality and Human Rights Commission, "Equal pay audit for larger organisations", 19 February 2019, https://www.equalityhumanrights.com/en/multipage-

on the five-step plan, however, and is "designed to help organisations with 50 employees or more".

According to the EHRC's approach, nearly every British employer will have significant gender pay gaps because it considers that as a general rule pay differences of 5% or more, or any recurring differences of 3% or more, are significant and should be investigated further[10].

The Enforcement Policy for the Gender Pay Gap Reporting

In March 2018, the EHRC published its enforcement policy: "Closing the gap: Enforcing the gender pay gap regulations"[11]. It says:

> In the context of the [Regulations], we have adopted the following principles:
>
> - We will seek to ensure high levels of compliance by raising awareness of the [Regulations]. Before the end of the first [gender pay gap] reporting year, in association with the Government Equalities Office (GEO), we will promote awareness, consulting with stakeholders on this policy and signposting employers to sources of information so that they develop an understanding of what is required under the [Regulations] and the benefits of compliance.
> - We will act consistently and aim to secure compliance by all employers subject to the [Regulations].
> - We are committed to openness and transparency, and aim in this policy to provide a detailed outline of the action that

guide/equal-pay-audit-larger-organisations

10 https://www.equalityhumanrights.com/en/multipage-guide/equal-pay-audit-step-4-causes-gender-pay-differences

11 Equality and Human Rights Commission, "Closing the gender pay gap: Enforcing the gender pay gap regulations", March 2018, https://www.equalityhumanrights.com/sites/default/files/gender-pay-gap-enforcing-the-regulations-march-2018.pdf

may be taken if employers do not comply with the [Regulations].

- We will use our enforcement powers firmly, promptly and effectively in the enforcement of the [Regulations]. In doing so we will act proportionately by corresponding with non-compliant employers before taking formal enforcement action. We have adopted timeframes within which we expect non-compliance to be resolved and which we believe all employers should be able to comply with.
- If we need to take enforcement action, we will inform employers why we are doing so, why we have chosen any particular course of action and what the next steps in the process will be. We will only use the more serious of our enforcement powers where employers fail to engage with us following our initial correspondence.
- We will maintain consistency in our approach to enforcement of the [Regulations] by requiring all staff members who make decisions about regulatory action to follow this policy.
- We will publish details of enforcement action that we take where we are obliged to do so under the [Equality Act] 2006, and when it is lawful and appropriate to do so.

The gist of the EHRC's policy for enforcing the Regulations is that it aims to "promote compliance without the need for formal enforcement". They said, "In 2018/19, we will aim to initiate enforcement action against all employers who have not reported their pay gap data," although the EHRC also had "the means to identify employers who submit statistically improbable data and will consider taking action against them where it is reasonable and proportionate to do so."

Further, the EHRC said:

> Where an employer does not comply with the [Regulations] by the relevant reporting date, we will write to them after the reporting date. The letter will:
>
> - draw their attention to their obligations under the [Regulations]
> - require them to comply with the [Regulations] retrospectively for the past reporting year within 28 days of our letter, and
> - require them to comply with the [Regulations] on or before the relevant reporting date in the current reporting year.
>
> We will then monitor the employer's compliance for both the past reporting year and the current reporting year. Where the employer complies, no further enforcement action will be taken in respect of those reporting years.

The EHRC's policy is that if non-compliance continued after initial correspondence, they would carry out an investigation into whether the employer had breached the law, in accordance with section 20 and schedule 2 to the Equality Act 2006. An employer which is investigated by the EHRC can expect it to provide the employer with draft terms of reference for the investigation and allow the employer or their nominated legal representative 14 days to make written representations about the draft terms of reference; consider any representations and publish the final terms of reference within the next 14 days; gather and analyse any relevant evidence, including representations from third parties (likely to be employees or external payroll or human resources consultants in most cases) within 14 days; provide a draft report within 14 further days; give the employer 28 days to make representations about the draft report; consider those representations before publishing the final report within 14 days. The whole investigation process is intended to take less than 14 weeks.

If the EHRC seeks an undertaking from an employer under section 23 of the Equality Act 2006, it is likely to require retrospective compliance with the Regulations for the previous reporting year by an agreed date, and reporting for the current gender pay gap reporting year to be made on time.

Under the EHRC policy, if an employer gave an undertaking under section 23 and then did not comply with it, the EHRC would apply to the county court in England or Wales, or the sheriff court in Scotland, for an order under section 24 of the Equality Act 2006 to comply with the undertakings which the employer had given to the EHRC.

The EHRC stated that if it concluded that an employer had breached the Regulations, then it would issue an unlawful act notice under section 21, requiring the employer to prepare a draft action plan within 13 days, setting out how the employer was going to remedy the continuing breach of the Regulations and avoid future breaches. If the employer did not prepare an action plan in those circumstances, then the EHRC said that it would apply for a court order requiring the employer do prepare an action plan within a specified timeframe. If the employer did provide an action plan, under the policy the EHRC would either approve it or issue a further unlawful act notice stating that the action plan was inadequate, requiring a revised action plan, and, if necessary, apply for a court order to enforce the second unlawful act notice. Failing to comply with a court order obtained by the EHRC to enforce the Regulations would be an offence by the employer liable to a Level 5 fine, the value of which is unlimited.

The Report on the 2018 Reporting Cycle

The EHRC Report "Closing the gender pay gap"[12] was published 14 December 2018 and at the outset states that as the body with responsibility for enforcing the Equality Act 2010, it must monitor and enforce the Regulations. It is not reported whether the EHRC received information from Her Majesty's Revenue and Customs or Companies House or, if not, how else the EHRC drew up the list of British employers subject to the gender pay gap reporting obligations under the Regulations. The EHRC assessed a sample of 440 organisational gender pay gap reports made under the Regulations for the 2017-2018 reporting year, however, there is no evidence that the EHRC undertook or required any internal financial auditing of the accuracy of the gender pay gap information which employers presented in 2018. It appears that the EHRC report took the gender pay gap figures provided by all employers at face value, unless the figures were blatantly statistically improbable. Independent analysis by the human resources commercial analytics firm, Staffmetrix, of the gender pay gap information presented by October 2018 for the reporting year 2018-2019 found that a quarter was non-compliant[13]. Indeed, nine percent was "statistically improbable", which the firm had also identified as a problem in the 2017-2018 reporting year.

According to the EHRC:

> All organisations subject to the regulations had published the relevant data by 1 August 2018 (and 94% had done so by the deadline for submission). Over three-quarters (77%) of organisations reported a median gender pay gap in favour of men; 14% in fa-

12 Equality and Human Rights Commission, "Closing the gender pay gap", 14 December 2018, https://www.equalityhumanrights.com/sites/default/files/closing-the-gender-pay-gap_0.pdf

13 Ashleigh Webber, "One in four gender pay gap reports non-compliant", Personnel Today, 16 October 2018, https://www.personneltoday.com/hr/non-compliant-gender-pay-gap-reports-2018-19/

vour of women; and in 9% of cases there was no reported median gender pay gap.

Given the crude and limited gender pay gap data required by the Regulations and the absence of any investigations or inquiries into any employer's gender pay gap information by the EHRC, it is unsurprising that the EHRC was able to make only general comments. The EHRC noted:

> ...this data alone does not give us any information about the possible causes of any of the pay gaps. Publishing an accompanying narrative report is a valuable opportunity for employers to publicly set out the reasons for any gaps and also to explain what they intend to do through a time-bound and target-driven action plan. Publishing accompanying narrative reports and action plans can help employers to:
>
> - attract and retain employees through a visible commitment to addressing the gender pay gap that showcases the organisation as fair and progressive
> - communicate a positive statement of intent to customers, shareholders and other stakeholders, helping to enhance reputation and brand, and
> - provide the basis of meaningful employee engagement on the gender pay gap, building trust and securing buy-in for any proposed solutions.

The EHRC further observed that a survey (published by the EHRC in October 2018) revealed that "over 60% of women would be more likely to apply for a job with an employer with a lower pay gap".

In 2018, only around half of the employers subject to the Regulations had chosen to publish a narrative account, with employers with fewer than 499 employees being least likely to do so. The EHRC stated its strong belief that "all employers should be required by law to publish a narrative report setting out the organisational context, current activity and future plans alongside their gender pay gap figures."

Of those employers who did produce narrative reports to accompany their gender pay gap reporting, some of these "were high level and contained very little detail or clear commitments to future action". Similarly, only 48% had published an equal pay action plan. Narrative reports tended to highlight distinct issues which affected their industry sector, as excuses, rather than to explain how they would address the mainstream reasons for pay inequality. For example, football clubs were keen to explain that very high salaries for male footballers were the cause of large gender pay gaps in their organisation[14]. The EHRC also noted that several reports simply "made generic commitments to existing initiatives to promote gender equality, such as the Women in Finance Charter".

Only 20% of employers in the sample had produced an identifiable action plan which was time-bound and included target-driven activities, however, only around half of those had fixed targets which would enable them to measure the progress of their plans year-on-year.

The EHRC summarised the themes which frequently appeared in the narrative reports provided by employers. Around half had mentioned activities aimed at improving their practice on recruitment, development and promotion, such targeting a broader range of recruitment events or partnering with existing women's networks in their industry sector. Some employers reported using positive role models of women who worked in male-dominated jobs, including senior management, or developing networks internally for women or minority employees. Most employers focused solely on equal pay for women at senior levels in the organisation, and only a few proposed action to improve women's career progression across the wider organisation.

14 Lewes Football Club is the first and currently the sole professional or semi-professional football club to pay its women's team the same as its men's team: Lewes Football Club, "Equality FC – a level playing field for women", 16 November 2018, https://www.lewesfc.com/article/equality-fc-a-level-playing-field-for-women

Unconscious bias training was frequently mentioned, however, EHRC research "has shown that the evidence base for this activity as a means of effectively addressing inequality is mixed."

More practical ways of reducing bias in recruitment which employers mentioned included anonymising curriculum vitae and application forms, ensuring that the language in job advertisements did not suggest a preference for male or female applicants and ensuring an equal number of men and women on interview panels. The EHRC says that evidence exists to show that effective actions to improve recruitment practices for women are having a balance of men and women on interview panels; increasing the number of women on shortlists for interviews; using skill-based recruitment tasks; and conducting structured interviews.

Another common technique was to refer to offering flexible working and enhanced shared parental leave, however, few specific details were included, with employers simply making more general, high-level commitments in a platitudinous way. The EHRC report says, "It is important that these practices are introduced alongside a culture where flexible working is understood as a valued way to retain and promote the contribution of skilled female staff, and to allow men to share parental duties". Only a small number of employers recorded plans to enhance payment for shared parental leave in order to encourage more fathers to share childcare, with most employers simply planning communication activity about the statutory rights.

In the EHRC sample, only two employers explicitly referred to taking "positive action", which is permitted by sections 158 and 159 of the Equality Act 2010. No employer expressed a plan to use section 159, sometimes known as the "tiebreak provision", which permits an employer to recruit or promote a woman, where women are under-represented or disadvantaged in the workforce by their sex, where a male and female candidate are equally qualified for the role.

In regard to positive action, the ACAS/GEO Guidance says:

Consider taking positive action

Under the Equality Act, an employer can take what the law terms 'positive action' to help employees or job applicants it thinks:

- are at a disadvantage because of their sex, and/or
- are under-represented in the organisation, or whose participation in the organisation is disproportionately low, because of their sex and/or
- have specific needs connected to their sex.
- This is a valuable tool for employers seeking to reduce their gender pay gap, particularly where they wish to remove obstacles deterring female employees from applying for jobs or promotions.

An employer taking positive action must show specific evidence that any positive action is both reasonably considered and appropriate and will not discriminate against others. Where this is the case, an employer may legally:

- take proportionate steps to remove any barriers or disadvantages
- provide support, training and encouragement to increase the participation of female employees.

There is no legal necessity for an employer to take positive action if it does not wish to do so.

In my view, the positive action provisions in the Equality Act 2010 have been so little used because in reality most recruitment exercises, particularly at senior levels, are greatly influenced by subjective considerations which give employers a very wide discretion lawfully to appoint or not appoint a woman, according to their personal preferences. Conversely, many employers are, perhaps rightly, extremely anxious that they may inadvertently breach equalities law if they attempt to take positive action[15].

Only 10% of employers in the sample focused on gender pay gaps in bonuses or performance-related pay and only a few talked about introducing greater levels of transparency in regard to bonuses. A notable exception was an employer in the manufacturing sector which had a bonus pay gap of 75% but committed to introducing greater transparency of rewards, including salary, bonus, and flexible benefits.

Similarly, only a small minority of employers mentioned apprenticeships as an area for action, despite the occupational segregation which affects them. A notable exception was an employer in the transport sector which committed to signing the Young Women's Trust Apprenticeship Pledge[16] and producing an action plan to increase the number of its women apprentices within the next year. Other employers described plans to improve education and training to encourage more women into occupationally-segregated areas of work, including early in their careers.

The EHRC wrote, with some irony:

> The low number of employers conducting or stating an intention to conduct equal pay audits was surprising given how many employers claimed in their narrative reports that their gender pay gap did not reflect any problems with equal pay… Some of these organisations may have conducted an equal pay audit but did not include it in the narrative report.

---

15 See, for example, Furlong v Chief Constable of Cheshire Police, Case 2405577/18, Liverpool Employment Tribunal, in which intended positive action was held to constitute unlawful direct sexual orientation, race and sex discrimination against a heterosexual, white, male applicant

16 Young Women's Trust, "Employer Pledge", https://www.youngwomenstrust.org/employerpledge

In its Report, the EHRC lists many sensible and practical "Ideas for Action":

Recruitment, development and promotion

- anonymising CVs and application forms
- introducing transparent recruitment and promotion procedures
- adopting a structured approach to interviewing
- including mixed-sex interview panels
- providing a clear brief, including diversity targets, to any recruitment consultants and executive search firms
- reaching the widest possible candidate pool through using a range of advertising methods and positive action
- introducing women's networks to develop peer support across the organisation
- developing mentoring schemes for women to build skills and encourage development

Flexible working

- advertise jobs at all levels as open to flexible working from day one
- promote a wide range of flexible working practices
- trial new ways of working
- be transparent and clear about the types of flexible working the organisation has considered, offered and granted
- showcase examples where flexible working is successful at a range of levels across the organisation

Caring and shared parental leave

- actively promote shared parental leave to staff

- consider enhancing the statutory minimum paternity leave – more generous and equal schemes operate in other countries and this has encouraged take-up among men
- incorporate flexibility into job design to encourage new parents to consider sharing caring responsibilities beyond the first year of their child's life

Apprenticeships

- promoting 'role models' from the business in liaison with schools and colleges, and placing advertisements for careers or work with skills agencies
- developing short programmes that allow young people to sample different types of apprenticeships
- offering flexible working in apprenticeships
- using positive action in apprenticeships

Positive action under section 158 of the Equality Act 2010

Bonuses and performance-related pay

- conducting an equal pay audit to uncover and remedy unequal pay for equal work, for example in
    - starting salaries
    - performance management systems
    - market supplements
    - pay protection
    - eligibility for bonuses and allowances

Monitoring data

- collecting and analysing a wider range of information than is required under the Equality Act 2010 (Gender Pay Gap Information) Regulations 2017, such as,

- recruitment processes, including the proportion of men and women applying, being shortlisted for and appointed to posts
- starting pay for men and women
- promotion rates for men and women
- retention rates for pregnant employees
- the proportion of mothers returning after maternity leave, and those still in employment two years after returning
- the proportion of men and women using various flexible working patterns, and levels within the organisation at which take-up is occurring
- whether pay gaps exist for part-time workers

The EHRC has statutory responsibility for enforcing the protections contained in the Equality Act 2010, including women workers' right to equal pay for equal work. Her Majesty's Revenue and Customs, which already has extensive regulatory responsibilities, knowledge and insight in regard to income arising from employment, currently has no role in enforcing gender pay gap transparency or the right to equal pay for equal work. No doubt due to austerity cuts to its budget and its wide range of equality, diversity and human rights responsibilities, the EHRC is taking very limited enforcement action to ensure compliance with the Regulations.

After tactfully mentioning the enforcement role of the EHRC, the ACAS/GEO Guidance points out:

> Employers will also run a reputational risk if they fail to publish the information, and in many cases the suspicions behind why an employer failed to publish their gender pay gap could have a negative impact and be far worse than what the report would have shown.

The biggest reputational and commercial risk to an employer which does not comply with the Regulations is not legal enforcement action by the EHRC but the potential damage to its relationships with employees, customers or clients, suppliers and industry partners, which could arise if its non-compliance becomes a matter of public knowledge and interest.

CHAPTER NINE
BEYOND COMPLIANCE TO BEST PRACTICE

Summary: In this chapter, I ask why and how an employer should move beyond compliance with the Equality Act 2010 (Gender Pay Gap Information) Regulations 2017 to best practice in closing the gender pay gap in its workforce, by considering the real experiences of Pay-Gaps.com and GoCompare.

Why Should an Employer Invest in Closing the Gender Pay Gap?

There are many principled reasons for wishing to eliminate unjustified pay gaps in the workforce, whether an employer is a follower of John Rawls' social justice model[1], Richard Posner's law and economics model[2], or another legal or political philosopher. At current rates of progress, the gender pay gap in the UK will take 55 years to close, for the "average" woman, whatever that means in real life. For the "average" BAME woman or the "average" disabled woman, closing the gender pay gap will take far longer than 55 years, to give just two examples of the importance of avoiding overlooking intersections of privilege and disadvantage in employment. Indeed, the "average" British woman and the "average" director responsible for setting pay policy in his organisation will probably be dead in 55 years' time.

There are sound business reasons to invest in closing the gender pay gap in our own organisations during our own lifetimes. Recruiting, training and retaining staff with the necessary skills and potential is a challenge for most employers and women workers remain a force whose capabilit-

---

1 John Rawls, "A Theory of Justice", Oxford University Press, 1972

2 Richard Posner, "Economic Analysis of Law", Boston: Little, Brown & Company, 1973

ies to contribute to the British labour market have not been fully tapped. Bridging the gender pay gap in the British labour market could create an extra £150 billion of GDP by 2025[3].

Anthony Horrigan, Chief Executive Officer of PayGaps.com, leads a data analytics business which specialises in gender pay gap reporting. He says about the Regulations, "All things being equal, gender pay gap reporting is nothing more than a mathematical exercise to be carried out, the results of which can be published and forgotten until the process recurs the following year. Cynical maybe, but only 32% of the initial 1,000 submissions mentioned any type of action plan this year. By 2025 millennials will account for 75% of the workforce and the majority have a very different view on diversity to the previous generation. Millennials consider the culture and social purpose of an organisation when evaluating places to work. An employer who persists in producing nothing but a statutory report will find it increasingly more difficult to attract and retain the best talent. When this is coupled with the fact that we are at the start of a demographic shift in the typical profile of an investor (moving towards women in their 40-50s), then it is clear to see that compliant-only employers will also find it more difficult to attract investment."

Anthony argues that for real insight-driven progress, an employer must push beyond compliance and that gender pay gap transparency amounts to no more than a doctor recording a sick patient's symptoms without prescribing any treatment. His work has led him to believe that radical change is required. He says, "To successfully mitigate bias and encourage a shift in culture and purpose the DNA of an organisation must be recoded. These fundamental changes must be led from the top of the organisation and a proper analysis of the current system should be carried out in a transparent way. The work should be far-reaching and look to uncover evidence from processes such as: a fair pay review (gender, ethnicity, disability, sexual orientation gaps), CEO pay ratio

3 McKinsey, "The Power of Parity: Advancing Women's Equality in the UK and OECD", 2016

review, recruitment funnel analysis, promotion, employee engagement and leadership / mentor practices."

In addition, Anthony calls for a full audit of human resources and pay policies in an organisation and an assessment of how transparent these policies are externally. He considers that if only 2% of the workforce are using an employer's flexible working policy, then that is evidence that the policy is not good enough, given the shift in the British labour market towards agile working. For example, he believes that when candidates cannot see parental leave policies on a prospective employer's website, they simply will avoid applying for roles[4].

PayGaps.com strongly advise their clients not to confine work on closing the gender pay gap to the Human Resources department. Anthony says, "A multi-departmental committee should be empowered, and progress led from the very top of the organisation. Gender pay gap reporting is not about paying or promoting women a bit more. It is about recoding parts of an organisation's DNA to allow it to inform, attract and retain a diverse family of humans that all work towards a clearly articulated organisational and social purpose that is supported and rewarded from the boardroom down."

I wanted to know which British employers had most seriously embraced the challenge of closing their gender pay gap. Given the significance of childcare and domestic responsibilities, part-time working and occupational segregation for the gender pay gap in Britain, I decided to find out which British employer was offering the longest period of maternity leave on full pay.

---

4 See further, Harini Iyengar, "To achieve workplace equality, employers have to start being transparent about fundamental employment rights", i-News, 17 September 2018, https://inews.co.uk/opinion/comment/to-achieve-workplace-equality-employers-have-to-start-being-transparent-about-fundamental-employment-rights/

Statutory rights to maternity, paternity and parental leave and pay in the UK are complicated[5], limited, different for mothers from fathers and, unlike parental entitlements under European Union law, UK entitlements are based on a paradigm in which childcare is first and foremost women's work[6]. In UK law, a father's right to care for his children is parasitic on the unavailable mother's right, rather than a parental right of his own.

An eligible female employee who has a baby is entitled to up to six weeks of statutory maternity pay at 90% of her average weekly earnings before tax, followed by up to 33 weeks at 90% of her average weekly earnings before tax, or £148.68[7] a week, whichever is the lower, from which income tax and National Insurance contributions are then deducted. Statutory paternity pay is available for an eligible male em-

5 Employment Rights Act 1996, sections 71-75; Maternity and Parental Leave etc Regulations 1999 (SI 1999/3312); Social Security Contributions and Benefits Act 1992; Statutory Maternity Pay (General) Regulations 1986 (SI 1986/1960); Paternity and Adoption Leave Regulations 2002 (SI 2002/2788); Statutory Paternity Pay and Statutory Adoption Pay (General) Regulations 2002 (SI 20022822); Statutory Paternity Pay and Statutory Adoption Pay (Weekly Rates) Regulations 2002 (SI 2002/2818); Children and Families Act 2014; Shared Parental Leave Regulations 2014 (SI 2014/3050); Statutory Shared Parental Pay (General) Regulations 2014 (SI 2014/3051); Maternity and Adoption Leave (Curtailment of Statutory Rights to Leave) Regulations 2014 (SI 2014/3052); Maternity Allowance (Curtailment) Regulations 2014 (SI 2014/3053); Statutory Maternity Pay and Statutory Adoption Pay (Curtailment) Regulations 2014 (SI 2014/3054); Employment Rights Act 1996 (Application of Sections 75G and 75H to Adoptions from Overseas) Regulations 2014 (SI 2014/3091); Shared Parental Leave and Paternity and Adoption Leave (Adoptions from Overseas) Regulations 2014 (SI 2014/3092); Statutory Shared Parental Pay (Adoption from Overseas) Regulations 2014 (SI 2014/3093); Statutory Shared Parental Leave and Pay (Persons Abroad and Mariners) Regulations 2014 (SI 2014/3134); Paternity, Adoption and Shared Parental Leave (Parental Order Cases) Regulations 2014 (SI 2014/3096); etc.

6 See Harini Iyengar, "Equal rights for men: The advent of the Children and Families Act may see working fathers push for parity with mothers", The Lawyer, 19 May 2014; Capital Customer Management Limited v Ali [2018] UKEAT 0161_17_1104; and Hextall v Chief Constable of Leicestershire Police [2017] UKEAT/0139/17/DA

7 The rate prior to 7 April 2019 is £145.18

ployee who has a baby for up to two weeks, at 90% of his average weekly earnings before tax, or £148.68 a week, whichever is the lower, from which income tax and National Insurance contributions are then deducted. Equivalent statutory entitlements are available for same sex couples, and for parents through adoption or surrogacy, with one partner obliged to take on the role of secondary parent, which UK law imposes on the father as between heterosexual birth parents. The shared parental leave rules allow a mother to curtail and then "share" with her partner some or all of the 39 weeks' paid leave which is treated by law as belonging to her[8].

Since the statutory entitlements to maternity, paternity and parental pay are so low in the UK, many employers offer contractual maternity, paternity and parental pay at a rate enhanced above the statutory minimum. The campaign organisation Pregnant Then Screwed[9] pointed me in the direction of GoCompare, a trailblazing business which offers nine months' leave on full pay for both mothers and fathers, and which I understand to be the longest period of leave on full pay offered by any British employer at the time of writing. I found out why they had chosen to go beyond compliance with their legal obligations towards best practice.

---

8 Compulsory maternity leave is two weeks long (Employment Rights Act 1996, section 72, and Maternity and Parental Leave Etc Regulations 1999 (SI 1999/3312), regulation 8), but factory workers have four weeks of compulsory maternity leave under the Public Health Act 1936, section 250. A father is unlikely to wish to take shared parental leave during the mother's compulsory maternity leave, since he would most commonly be using his two weeks of paternity leave at this time.

9 http://pregnantthenscrewed.com/

The GoCompare Group plc[10] ("GoCo") operates in the FinTech and financial services sectors, areas of the British labour market which have traditionally had worse than average gender pay gaps[11]. GoCo has an expanding workforce of 299, made up of 125 females (42%) and 174 males (58%). It has collected data on equal pay for a number of years, and Alex Currie, Human Resources Director, says, "As an employer we strive for equal pay for equal work. It is important for us to ensure that those doing the same or similar roles with the same amount of experience and skill are remunerated equally because it is the right thing to do."

GoCo used to offer maternity leave, shared parental leave or adoption leave consisting of full pay for three months with a further three months at half pay, and paternity leave of two weeks at full pay, already in excess of the statutory requirements. Alex says, "Whilst we understand we're above average in terms of the proportion of women in our Tech community, we always strive to do better. One of our ways to support this is to widen the scope of benefits we offer to our employees, making us an appealing employer to parents, and an exemplar in the South Wales employment market."

---

10 GoCompare Group operates GoCompare, a leading UK financial services, utilities and home services comparison website; MyVoucherCodes, which is a digital media affiliate marketing specialist that connects consumers with money saving offer's from the world's leading brands; Energylinx, an established energy switching and comparison service with more energy supplier relationships than any other UK comparison provider; and weflip, an innovative switching service that uses technology to automatically flip people on to cheap energy tariffs, forever.

11 See, for example, Haroon Siddique, "City's 'shocking' gender pay gap revealed in equality report," The Guardian, 9 April 2009 reporting on Equality and Human Rights Commission report: https://www.equalityhumanrights.com/en/publication-download/research-report-14-pay-gaps-across-equality-strands (1 April 2009); and Caitlin Morrison, "Gender pay gap hits 91% for financial services workers earning more than £1m a year", The Independent, 13 May 2018, https://www.independent.co.uk/news/business/news/gender-pay-gap-men-women-salary-financial-services-one-million-pounds-salary-a8347141.html reporting research by Fox & Partners LLP

The Diversity and Inclusion Committee organised an investigative parenting workshop, held with existing and prospective parents at Go-Compare, aiming to understand what mattered most to their employees. Alex says, "Listening to our staff it became clear that there is an internal struggle between coming back to work due to financial pressure and spending time at home with a new baby. We wanted our working parents to take the question out of the equation. Just because we were not required to legally, doesn't mean we don't want to as an organisation." The business responded with a bold policy which evidences their belief in the capabilities and commitment of their working parent employees and their choice to provide working parent employees with the best workplace possible. GoCo's starting point is that if an employer genuinely wants women at the top of the business, it needs to attract them.

GoCo's Enhanced Parental Leave Policy ensures parity across all parental groups. It enables employees who wish to take maternity leave, shared parental leave or adoption leave to receive nine months of leave at full pay.

Ellen Sugden, Risk and Compliance Director, fed into the investigative workshop and is currently taking nine months' adoption leave. She says, "I am pleased they listened to the variety of issues prospective parents face. Adoption leave can be slightly different and uncertain, which is why having HR support, and acceptance about the challenges we face, is so refreshing. As the main earner in our family, nine months' full pay takes the pressure off financially, whilst also making the individual feel supported in their wish to take nine months off with their children."

The GoCo enhanced paternity policy now provides fathers and secondary care-givers with four weeks' paternity leave at full-pay and flexibility over when they use their extra two weeks' leave. Mike Blackburn, GoCo Group Financial Controller, who is expecting his first baby, says, "I am going to take two weeks initially and then spread the other two weeks over the rest of the year. It's great to have this flexibility and support from my employer. Most people I know have only had two weeks' paternity, so four weeks is generous and will enable me to spend more time with the baby over a longer period of time."

GoCo believes that their Enhanced Parental Leave Policy contributes to their talent acquisition and retention strategy, ensuring that they attract and keep senior women, for the benefit of the business. It is the first in a number of changes to their policies and procedures as part of their wider diversity and inclusion strategy.

Alex tells me, "We have taken many steps to tackle the gender pay gap; we launched our GoFurther academy in 2018 which offers sponsored degrees without debt, graduate schemes, internships, apprenticeships and work experience, enabling the existing workforce and prospective students to develop and progress. Our staff make GoCo the brilliant business that it is, so we like to make sure they're looked after. By launching the academy, we're able to offer our talented bunch even more opportunities for development so they're able to expand their range of expertise, knowledge and competencies, reaching their highest potential."

In 2018, GoCo updated its approach to recruitment, operating blind curriculum vitae (from which the name and other details which could identify the applicant's gender are removed) across all roles to eliminate unconscious bias. They also use the anti-gender-bias software "Textio" for all job advertisements to ensure they are appealing to a diverse cross-section of candidates. In addition, their job advertisements actively promote flexible working patterns.

In conjunction with Innovation Point, GoCo launched a Women in Tech breakfast in South Wales in 2019, which is a collective of women at various points in their careers, benefiting from a mentoring programme.

Since introducing their Enhanced Parental Leave Policy, GoCo have seen 100% uptake from employees on maternity leave, with 13 mothers taking advantage of the full nine months' maternity leave on full pay in 2018. Interest in shared parental leave from male employees has increased, with their first shared parental leave participant in 2018. They also have two extended adoption leaves taking place in 2019.

During the recruitment process, GoCompare frequently receive positive feedback on the generosity of their family friendly schemes, particularly their openness to consider reduced-hour roles, job shares or flexible working. Alex believes, "Our family friendly policies encourage more females to consider GoCompare as a place of work. Across 2018, female applicants increased by 10% and appear to continue to be on the rise in 2019."

Consideration of the insights which PayGaps.com have gained from working with employers which are auditing their gender pay gaps, and the practical experiences at GoCo demonstrates to me that there does not have to be any conflict between effective business strategy and employers making the choice to move beyond compliance with their minimum statutory obligations towards the best practice which can reduce their gender pay gaps.

CHAPTER TEN
CONCLUSION

Summary: I conclude that equal pay litigation and sex discrimination litigation will not close the gender pay gap; that the Equality Act 2010 (Gender Pay Gap Information) Regulations 2017 will not close the gender pay gap; and that the necessary statutory programme will not occur in the near future. Therefore, the change must come from employers and workers themselves.

Unfairnesses and barriers to equal opportunities in the workplace between men and women create inefficiencies in the British labour market. Moreover, the right to equal pay for equal work and the right to just and favourable remuneration ensuring for herself and her family an existence worthy of human dignity, supplemented, if necessary, by other means of social protection, are universal human rights.

British women have had, on paper, the right to equal pay for equal work since 1970. They have had the rights to protection against unlawful sex discrimination at work and to bring equal pay claims since 1975. Nevertheless, in addition to unlawful unequal pay, the gender pay gap remains widespread and persistent. Current equal pay law places the burden on each individual woman to sue her employer for breach of contract to enforce her right to equal pay, in a jurisdiction which is a technical minefield. Equal pay litigation and sex discrimination litigation by individual women will not close the gender pay gap. The EHRC's capacity to fund or to intervene in test cases which could advance the development of equal pay law, to undertake outreach work, or to enforce the Regulations have been heavily restricted by budget cuts caused by austerity policies which followed the 2008 financial crisis.

The Office for National Statistics used sophisticated regression modelling to explore the factors which contribute to the gender pay gap[1]. The gender pay gap remains entirely in favour of men for all occupations. Those occupations with the smallest gender pay gap have almost equal employment shares between men and women. Generally, the longer someone remains in the workforce, the more skilled and experienced they become. However, women's pay growth in respect of age was lower than men's. Women's pay also stopped growing at a younger age. The gender pay gap for full-time workers widens after 40 and peaks between ages 50 and 59.

Yet, the most striking point in the ONS analysis is that only 36.1% of the difference in men's and women's hourly pay could be explained by differences in personal and job characteristics between men and women. The biggest factor explaining the gender pay gap in the British labour market was occupational segregation, which explained 23% of the gender pay gap.

---

1 Office for National Statistics, Tom Evans, "Understanding the gender pay gap in the UK", 17 January 2018, https://www.ons.gov.uk/employmentandlabourmarket/peopleinwork/earningsandworkinghours/articles/understandingthegenderpaygapintheuk/2018-01-17

Figure 13: The overall explained part and its components expressed as a percentage of the difference between log hourly earnings of men and women, UK, 2017

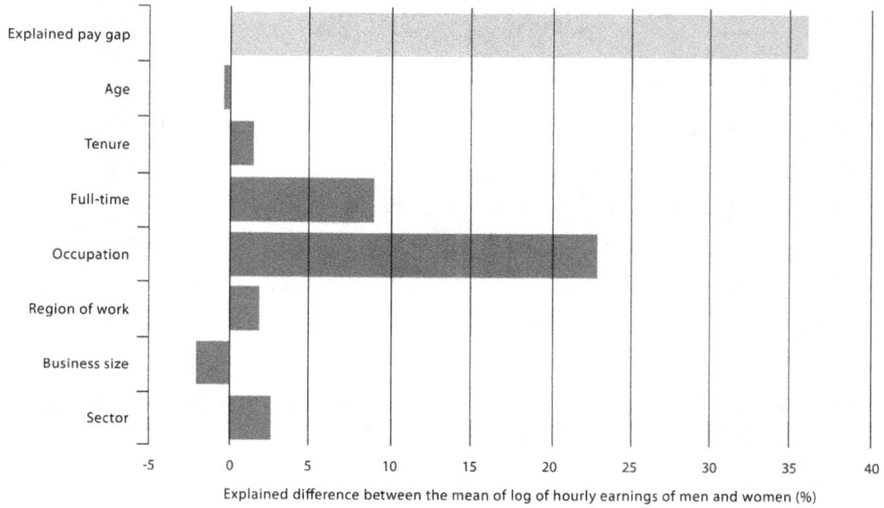

Source: Annual Survey of Hours and Earnings (ASHE) – Office for National Statistics

As the ONS tactfully say, the remaining 63.9% of the gender pay gap in the labour market remains: unexplained. It would be statistically improper to conclude that the explanation for the remaining 63.9% of the gender pay gap must be unlawful unequal pay, but that explanation was not excluded by the ONS's modelling either.

At present, there is little legal incentive for any employer to invest in a serious and comprehensive equal pay audit, to understand why men and women in its workforce earn different pay, and or to acknowledge the intersections of disadvantage faced by women with other legally-protected characteristics or vulnerabilities as well as their sex. The commercial and reputational risks associated with public scrutiny created by gender pay gap reporting are threats for the largest and best-known employers only, and depend on the work of investigative financial journalists. Therefore, although gender pay gap transparency is a welcome step forward, the Regulations will not close the gender pay gap.

Fundamental changes to lift the range of barriers which hamper women's full participation in the British labour market[2] would require serious and co-ordinated action by Government.

In Iceland, every October since 1975, women have gone on strike for the day on Kvennafrídagurinn to demonstrate the indispensable work of women for Iceland's economy and society and to protest against the gender pay gap. Amendments to the Gender Equality Act No. 10/2008, which came into force in 2018, now require public and private companies to pay employees equally "regardless of gender, ethnicity, sexuality or nationality". Employers with 25 or more employees must in practice conduct a comprehensive job evaluation and equal pay audit of their workforce in order to obtain the certification necessary to prove that they offer equal pay for work of equal value[3].

At the time of writing, Britain is poised between a No Deal Brexit, a Withdrawal Agreement, various hypothetical withdrawal agreements which may be concluded, and the possibility of remaining in the European Union. Closing the gender pay gap in the British labour market does not appear to be a legislative priority in the UK as it is in Iceland. Therefore, the co-ordinated statutory programme necessary to close the gender pay gap is unlikely to occur in the near future.

If the gender pay gap is to close in our lifetimes, to benefit employers, workers and the wider British economy and society, then the change must come from employers and workers themselves. Please read this

2 For proposed policy solutions, see Women's Equality Party, "Women's Equality Party General Election Manifesto 2017", "Equal Pay", 2017 (see Appendix), and Harini Iyengar "To achieve workplace equality, employers have to start being transparent about fundamental employment rights", i-News, 17 September 2018, https://inews.co.uk/opinion/comment/to-achieve-workplace-equality-employers-have-to-start-being-transparent-about-fundamental-employment-rights/

3 Government of Iceland, Ministry of Finance and Economic Affairs and Prime Minister's Office, "Equal Pay Certification", 2019, https://www.government.is/topics/human-rights-and-equality/equal-pay-certification/

book and then ask yourself what positive actions you can take to close the gender pay gap in your own organisation.

AFTERWORD

Being paid a fair sum for a fair day's work is a fundamental aspect of the dignity of labour. As a barrister, I advise and represent employers, individuals and representative organisations in cases where injustice or unfairness may arise through poor implementation or enforcement of equal pay law or the law against sex discrimination. As a political activist, I campaign against sexist stereotypes and structural inequalities between males and females in British culture, including in our nurseries, schools, colleges, universities, apprenticeships, paid workforce, voluntary sector, and in unpaid work – which includes: childcare; care for older or disabled adults; cleaning; cooking, serving and clearing meals; laundry; housework; grocery shopping; buying, maintaining and washing children's clothes; household maintenance and repairs; arranging social outings and celebrations; household administration; and emotional care for loved ones. As a working mother, the self-employed lone parent of three children, and the family breadwinner, my own life is affected on a personal level by trends in the labour market, which makes pay equality an issue close to my heart, as well as a topic of legal and intellectual interest to me.

At the same time as exhorting you to take action for change, I do not want you read this book and become consumed with bitterness about unequal pay which you may have received in your own working life, or about your future job prospects in an imperfect labour market, which cannot match your potential and aspirations. Nor do I want you to read this book and become paralysed by guilt for your high pay or attractive work opportunities, which you may have received because of a privileged characteristic or status. At such moments, I advise you to take a pause and ponder the true value of wages in human life, and the other riches of human existence.

APPENDIX 'THE WOMEN'S EQUALITY PARTY MANIFESTO FOR THE GENERAL ELECTION 2017', EXTRACT ON EQUAL PAY[1]

For every hour they work women still earn just 81p of every £1 earned by men. There are many other ways of measuring the pay gap – pay for each worker, total pay for all women, and for all men – but however you measure it, the story is the same: 45 years after the Equal Pay Act, women earn less per hour, less per job and less overall than men.

Girls outperform boys in most academic subjects, yet too often fall behind in the workplace, hampered by conscious and unconscious bias and other obstacles. Men are almost twice as likely as women to become entrepreneurs, while women are routinely pushed towards low-paid, undervalued employment sectors and part-time roles with lower potential to progress. Women are under-represented in Science, Technology, Engineering and Maths (STEM) and our education system is not working to change this. The economy is losing out.

There has been a huge growth in female self-employment but, for many women, starting their own business is not a choice; it is a consequence of public sector job losses, increases in retirement age or driven by a need to balance unpaid caring with an income.

The pay gap widens for women after 50, and older women who have taken a career break to care for others struggle to get back into work. Women also more often retire into poverty because they are likely to have earned less than men and to have taken time away from work to

1 Women's Equality Party, General Election Manifesto 2017, pp 13-15, https://www.womensequality.org.uk/manifesto

meet caring responsibilities. On top of this, women are suffering as a result of changes to equalise retirement age that were imposed without allowing the women impacted sufficient time to plan for their retirement.

Women are disproportionately affected by cuts to services and by changes to social security which women rely on more than men. Over 85% of such cuts and changes affect women, and BAME women and disabled women are hit particularly hard.

In total, women earn just 52% of what men do every year because not only are they paid less, but they also are more likely to sacrifice opportunities for paid work for the sake of their family. While many parents choose to spend time at home with young children, at least 600,000 stay-at-home parents would prefer to work if they could afford to do so. The Women's Business Council has estimated in 2012 that there were 2.3 million women who wanted to be in work but were not, and a further 1.3 million who wanted to work more hours. Across the country working mothers of young children are effectively paying to work. This is not only bad for women and for the wider economy, it is bad for children.

The underfunding of the government's 30-hour free childcare scheme for working parents of three- and four-year-olds has resulted in nurseries not being able to sign up to it and 50,000 eligible children in England missing out. In the devolved nations, the situation is not much better, despite important efforts taken by the Scottish Parliament and Welsh and Northern Ireland Assemblies. Very few councils in Scotland have enough childcare capacity to meet the needs of working parents; Wales has the lowest rate of female employment across the UK; and in Northern Ireland half of all parents reduce their working hours or leave work altogether because of the cost of childcare.

WE are the only political party putting forward a solution that works for everyone and gives children the best possible start in life: universal free childcare, available from the end of shared parental leave. Other parties approach these vital issues piecemeal and without addressing the ways in which they are connected. Our plans will boost the economy, create up to 1.7 million jobs across the UK and save as much as £37 billion through higher tax revenues and lower benefit payments. Evidence shows that a 10% increase in the proportion of mothers working could raise £1.5 billion in increased tax revenue and reduced in-work benefits.

Overall, the contribution of women to our economy and our society is undervalued, both in paid work and at home. The OECD has shown that if we unleashed the true potential of women the economy could grow by an extra 10% by 2030, and McKinsey has estimated that bridging the UK gender gap in work would create an extra £150 billion on top of business-as-usual GDP forecasts by 2025. This could translate into 840,000 women getting to work and gaining financial independence.

It is time to end the occupational segregation and the pay bias for occupations perceived as "male" or "female" which means caring work is paid less than manual labour. Women who want to work should be able to do so and be paid fairly for it.

WE will:

- offer free childcare all across the UK from the end of paid parental leave at nine months. Childcare will be centrally funded but where decision-making is in the hands of devolved governments or local authorities, funds will depend on the provision meeting the criteria of being universal and not for profit. Parents who work non-traditional hours and need more flexible childcare will have the option of a voucher alternative;

- extend the recent requirement for gender pay reporting for businesses, organisations and public bodies with more than 250 employees to smaller businesses of 50 employees or more, and monitor the impact of the gender pay gap reporting in Scotland where public authorities with more than 20 employees are to be required to publish their gender pay gap;

- require gender pay gap reporting to be broken down by age, employment status, ethnicity, race, disability, industry and working hours, as well as gathering data on retention during – and up to a year after – parental leave;
- increase the capacity of public authorities to undertake an equal pay audit review, broken down by other protected characteristics, and publish the results, along with an action plan to close the gender pay gap and reduce occupational segregation. Define ways to expand this to all organisations contracting with the government;
- work with HM Revenue and Customs to gather data through PAYE and Self-Assessment forms on gender, age, race, ethnicity, disability status, industry and working hours. This data should be anonymised and published in an open data format to allow researchers to develop a comprehensive understanding of disparity in pay;
- remove barriers to justice for those who have suffered workplace discrimination by lowering the fee for issuing an employment claim from the current £250 to £50, and scrapping the hearing fee of £950 altogether. Monitor the Scottish Government's intention to abolish employment claim fees. Fee remissions for those on low incomes will remain in place;
- restore the power of employment tribunals to advise those employers who have been proven to discriminate;
- investigate the most appropriate way to introduce split Universal Credit payments to ensure women's financial independence;

- give new parents a longer grace period of nine months – rather than the current three months – for cases involving maternity discrimination or parental leave discrimination;
- activate the provisions of the 2010 Equality Act that permit dual discrimination claims;
- require the criteria that protect women from being made redundant while on maternity leave to be extended to pregnant women before they start maternity leave;
- require employers to provide time for, and a place where, women can breastfeed or express milk in the workplace;
- support the development of a fully qualified workforce in early years education with pay scales that are commensurate with the importance and value of pre-school and early years care;
- make pre- and after-school clubs available and affordable on school premises from 8am to 6pm;
- incentivise companies to put in place on-site childcare by exempting on-site childcare facilities from business rates, paid for by a small uplift in the rates for large premises;
- encourage detailed research into the experience of working women during the menopause, reducing stigma and spreading awareness among employers;
- build on the progress that has been made with the New State Pension and incentivise those on low pay to save – especially those in part-time work, who may miss out on the new "auto-enrolment" pensions;
- join forces with those who are calling for a new single rate of pension tax relief. It is not right that those on low pay, who are more likely to be women, get 20p back from the tax man when

they save while those on high pay, who are more likely to be men, get 40p back;

- honour the contract the WASPI women believe they entered into when they began paying National Insurance, and implement fair transitional pension arrangements for all women born in the 1950s;
- commission a public education campaign to raise awareness of the level of unpaid care work placed on women, and encourage men to share the load;
- hold businesses to a higher standard when they publish data on the gender pay gap so that they show the number of men and women working part-time, the number of BAME and disabled women, and retention rates before and after maternity leave; and
- ensure that the social security system works towards creating gender equality rather than increasing inequalities.

MORE BOOKS BY LAW BRIEF PUBLISHING

A selection of our other titles available now:-

'A Practical Guide to the Ending of Assured Shorthold Tenancies' by Elizabeth Dwomoh
'Commercial Mediation – A Practical Guide' by Nick Carr
'A Practical Guide to Financial Services Claims' by Chris Hegarty
'The Law of Houses in Multiple Occupation: A Practical Guide to HMO Proceedings' by Julian Hunt
'A Practical Guide to Unlawful Eviction and Harassment' by Stephanie Lovegrove
'A Practical Guide to Solicitor and Client Costs' by Robin Dunne
'Artificial Intelligence – The Practical Legal Issues' by John Buyers
'A Practical Guide to Wrongful Conception, Wrongful Birth and Wrongful Life Claims' by Rebecca Greenstreet
'Occupiers, Highways and Defective Premises Claims: A Practical Guide Post-Jackson – 2nd Edition' by Andrew Mckie
'A Practical Guide to Financial Ombudsman Service Claims' by Adam Temple & Robert Scrivenor
'A Practical Guide to the Law of Enfranchisement and Lease Extension' by Paul Sams
'A Practical Guide to Marketing for Lawyers – 2nd Edition' by Catherine Bailey & Jennet Ingram
'A Practical Guide to Advising Schools on Employment Law' by Jonathan Holden
'Certificates of Lawful Use and Development: A Guide to Making and Determining Applications' by Bob Mc Geady & Meyric Lewis
'A Practical Guide to the Law of Dilapidations' by Mark Shelton
'A Practical Guide to the 2018 Jackson Personal Injury and Costs Reforms' by Andrew Mckie
'A Guide to Consent in Clinical Negligence Post-Montgomery' by Lauren Sutherland QC
'A Practical Guide to Running Housing Disrepair and Cavity Wall Claims: 2nd Edition' by Andrew Mckie & Ian Skeate
'A Practical Guide to the General Data Protection Regulation (GDPR)' by Keith Markham
'A Practical Guide to Digital and Social Media Law for Lawyers' by Sherree Westell

'A Practical Guide to Holiday Sickness Claims – 2nd Edition' by Andrew Mckie & Ian Skeate
'A Practical Guide to Inheritance Act Claims by Adult Children Post-Ilott v Blue Cross' by Sheila Hamilton Macdonald
'A Practical Guide to Elderly Law' by Justin Patten
'Arguments and Tactics for Personal Injury and Clinical Negligence Claims' by Dorian Williams
'A Practical Guide to QOCS and Fundamental Dishonesty' by James Bentley
'A Practical Guide to Drone Law' by Rufus Ballaster, Andrew Firman, Eleanor Clot
'Practical Mediation: A Guide for Mediators, Advocates, Advisers, Lawyers, and Students in Civil, Commercial, Business, Property, Workplace, and Employment Cases' by Jonathan Dingle with John Sephton
'Practical Horse Law: A Guide for Owners and Riders' by Brenda Gilligan
'A Comparative Guide to Standard Form Construction and Engineering Contracts' by Jon Close
'A Practical Guide to Compliance for Personal Injury Firms Working With Claims Management Companies' by Paul Bennett
'A Practical Guide to the Landlord and Tenant Act 1954: Commercial Tenancies' by Richard Hayes & David Sawtell
'A Practical Guide to Personal Injury Claims Involving Animals' by Jonathan Hand
'A Practical Guide to Psychiatric Claims in Personal Injury' by Liam Ryan
'Introduction to the Law of Community Care in England and Wales' by Alan Robinson
'A Practical Guide to Dog Law for Owners and Others' by Andrea Pitt
'Ellis and Kevan on Credit Hire – 5th Edition' by Aidan Ellis & Tim Kevan
'RTA Allegations of Fraud in a Post-Jackson Era: The Handbook – 2nd Edition' by Andrew Mckie
'RTA Personal Injury Claims: A Practical Guide Post-Jackson' by Andrew Mckie
'On Experts: CPR35 for Lawyers and Experts' by David Boyle
'An Introduction to Personal Injury Law' by David Boyle
'A Practical Guide to Claims Arising From Accidents Abroad and Travel Claims' by Andrew Mckie & Ian Skeate

'A Practical Guide to Cosmetic Surgery Claims' by Dr Victoria Handley
'A Practical Guide to Chronic Pain Claims' by Pankaj Madan
'A Practical Guide to Claims Arising from Fatal Accidents' by James Patience
'A Practical Approach to Clinical Negligence Post-Jackson' by Geoffrey Simpson-Scott
'A Practical Guide to Personal Injury Trusts' by Alan Robinson
'Employers' Liability Claims: A Practical Guide Post-Jackson' by Andrew Mckie
'A Practical Guide to Subtle Brain Injury Claims' by Pankaj Madan
'The Law of Driverless Cars: An Introduction' by Alex Glassbrook
'A Practical Guide to Costs in Personal Injury Cases' by Matthew Hoe
'A Practical Guide to Alternative Dispute Resolution in Personal Injury Claims – Getting the Most Out of ADR Post-Jackson' by Peter Causton, Nichola Evans, James Arrowsmith
'A Practical Guide to Personal Injuries in Sport' by Adam Walker & Patricia Leonard
'The No Nonsense Solicitors' Practice: A Guide To Running Your Firm' by Bettina Brueggemann
'Baby Steps: A Guide to Maternity Leave and Maternity Pay' by Leah Waller
'The Queen's Counsel Lawyer's Omnibus: 20 Years of Cartoons from The Times 1993-2013' by Alex Steuart Williams

These books and more are available to order online direct from the publisher at www.lawbriefpublishing.com, where you can also read free sample chapters. For any queries, contact us on 0844 587 2383 or mail@lawbriefpublishing.com.

Our books are also usually in stock at www.amazon.co.uk with free next day delivery for Prime members, and at good legal bookshops such as Wildy & Sons.

We are regularly launching new books in our series of practical day-to-day practitioners' guides. Visit our website and join our free newsletter to be kept informed and to receive special offers, free chapters, etc.

You can also follow us on Twitter at www.twitter.com/lawbriefpub.

www.ingramcontent.com/pod-product-compliance
Lightning Source LLC
LaVergne TN
LVHW022037200926
848481LV00003B/713
9781911035947